VEAL COOKERY

BOOKS BY CRAIG CLAIBORNE

VEAL
·COOKERY·

Craig Claiborne/Pierre Franey

Drawings by Barbara Fiore
Photographs by Bill Aller

HARPER & ROW, PUBLISHERS

New York   Hagerstown   San Francisco   London

Portions of this material originally appeared in *The International Review of Food & Wine*.

Permission to reproduce numerous recipes that have appeared in *The New York Times* is gratefully acknowledged.

Designed by Stephanie Tevonian

Library of Congress Cataloging in Publication Data

Claiborne, Craig.
  Veal cookery.

  Includes index.
1. Cookery (Veal) I. Franey, Pierre, joint author. II. Title.
TX749.C58   641.6'6'2   78-2123
ISBN 0-06-010773-1

81   82   10   9   8   7   6   5   4   3   2

CONTENTS

ACKNOWLEDGMENT

Many of the recipes in this book were contributed by some of the finest restaurant owners and chefs throughout the world. We have freely adapted these recipes according to our own tastes and techniques, and it is our fond hope that those who were so obliging will be pleased with our efforts.

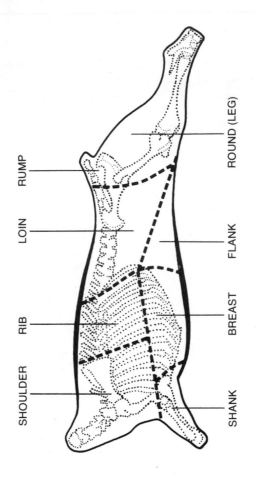

INTRODUCTION

Veal is, in the minds of connoisseurs, the most delicate, elegant, and delectable of meats. Ask any great professional chef who presides over a European kitchen and he will tell you that veal is also the most versatile of viands. The reasons why are not difficult to come by.

It is an established fact that some foods have a natural affinity for other foods and flavors. Salmon and fresh dill are a classic combination. Ground pork in the form of sausages or stuffings is enormously compatible with sage or fennel. Chicken can be especially tasty with rosemary or tarragon. And rosemary and lamb make a happy liaison. The Chinese combine soy sauce, garlic, and ginger in thousands of traditional dishes, just as the people of the Mediterranean regions rely heavily on dishes that combine tomatoes, garlic, and olive oil. Such happy blendings are virtually endless.

Veal, perhaps more than any other meat, has the uncommon ability to "marry well" with a limitless variety of other foods and flavors. A classic ossobuco always has what the Italians call a *gremolata*—a felicitous combination of garlic, parsley, and grated lemon peel. Veal is complemented by almost all the spices on the shelf, and there is almost no edible herb that veal does not adapt kindly to.

Oddly enough, veal also teams remarkably well with fish. Veal à la Oskar, named for a king of Sweden, is invariably made with crawfish, crabmeat, shrimp, or lobster. In vitello tonnato, one of the greatest inventions for summer dining, the veal is sauced with a cold dressing that contains tuna fish and anchovies.

Most of the great veal dishes of the world are of European origin, for veal is rarely found in the Middle and Far East. In this book, the Far East is represented, in fact, by only two recipes, both of which are those of T. T. Wang of the Shun Lee restaurants in Manhattan. He adapted them from European-style veal, using traditional Chinese flavorings, including green onions, garlic, chili paste with garlic, and ginger.

Many of the dishes included in this volume are the result of requests for veal recipes from restaurants both in America and Europe. All these recipes were carefully tested by us, and we freely made such changes as we deemed necessary or appropriate.

In preparing these dishes we were struck by several national patterns that are of passing interest. For reasons that are unaccountable, we noted that the Swedes have a way with ground veal dishes. Italians, of course, have a passion for veal in the form of scaloppine. Hungarians admire stews. And the French dote on what are known as the "odd parts"—the variety cuts of veal, such as sweetbreads, brains, liver, kidneys.

Incidentally, if you are calorie-conscious (we aren't, at least in any overt or missionary sense), veal is far less calorie-ridden then beef or pork. Perhaps the greatest low-calorie dish ever created is included in this book. It is for a paillarde of veal in which a flattened veal steak seasoned with salt and pepper is cooked briefly over charcoal or in a hot skillet. It has just a touch of butter at the end, which you could omit.

As with any other food, the quality of veal ranges from poor to superior, and the quality depends on how and what the calf is fed throughout its short lifetime.

Essentially, the veal sold in this country is of two sorts—the veal from milk-fed calves and the veal from grass-fed calves.

The finest veal—that from milk-fed calves—has a color of palest pink. The darker this color, the redder it becomes, the less desirable it is for home use. Some calves can legally be sold as veal although the meat may approach the color of fire-engine red.

Milk-fed veal is from calves that have been raised and fed in what is called the European tradition. Curiously, the United States was to a great extent responsible for the proliferation of veal produced in this manner.

Veal raising on a commercial scale started and accelerated in Europe in the early 1950s, thanks to a great degree to the American government. At that time there was a huge surplus of skim milk in this country, and it was shipped overseas at extremely low prices. This, according to one industry spokesman, put European veal production on the map. The European technique for feeding and raising calves was introduced in the United States less than twenty years ago.

Basically, the technique is as follows:

Calves are housed in stalls from the age of three or four days to fifteen weeks. During this period, they are fed a special formula made with dry milk solids—milk proteins blended with fats to compensate for the butter fat that has been removed. The milk solids are mixed with water and fed to the calves twice a day. With this diet, the calves attain a weight of 350 pounds at butchering age, a weight that is impossible to achieve with other techniques.

The production in this country of European-style veal is presently about 350,000 calves, which represents between ten and fifteen percent of the total veal consumption in America. The remainder is what is known as "bob" veal (pale in color and soft in texture, from calves less than a week old) and grass-fed veal, which is from calves several weeks old and, generally, lacking in that desirable cream-pink color. The producers of European-style veal predict that within a decade or so the majority of the veal in this country will be produced in the European way.

•Roasts•

When it comes to roasts of meat or poultry, there is many an epicure who will declare that nothing can equal a perfect roast of veal. People with sensitive palates—exquisite taste buds, if you will—generally find that a roast of beef has its own special qualities. After a while, however, these qualities begin to pall. Such a roast on successive occasions may very well yield to monotony. Roast lamb, which must be given a high rank in the hierarchy of gastronomy, may have too specialized a flavor for repetitive feasting. Roast game and roast turkey have justifiable moments of glory. But in the long run, nothing quite matches the perfection of veal fresh from the oven.

Oddly perhaps, a roast of veal, be it the leg, the rump, the saddle, or the loin, is remarkably easy to cook. It requires little attention in the oven—an occasional basting here and there—and the seasonings can be widely varied.

It must be said, however, that in this section is the single most complicated dish in the book. It is the one known as rognonnade of veal, and consists of wrapping the kidney and fillet of veal inside a boned loin. Although this is a bit difficult for the inexperienced home cook, it is by no means impossible. Properly done, it is a gastronomic triumph, fit for the tables of princes and kings, and even the likes of you and me. It is a highly festive dish and should be reserved for special occasions.

We have also included at the tail end of this section two main-course dishes that use leftover roast veal.

Rôti de Veau à la Crème

*(Roast veal in an herb
and cream sauce)*

6 or more servings

1 trussed, 3½-pound boneless rump veal roast, bones reserved
Salt and freshly ground pepper to taste
4 tablespoons butter
2 medium onions, about ¼ pound, peeled
2 carrots, about ¼ pound, scraped and cut into thin rounds

1 clove garlic, peeled
1 bay leaf
6 sprigs fresh thyme or 1 teaspoon dried
6 sprigs fresh tarragon or 1 teaspoon dried
1 cup heavy cream
1 tablespoon chopped fresh tarragon or 1 teaspoon dried

1. Preheat the oven to 350 degrees.

2. Sprinkle the roast with salt and pepper. Heat half the butter in a heavy skillet and, when it is hot, add the meat. Turn the meat in the butter to brown it lightly on all sides.

3. Slice the onions and scatter the slices around the meat. Add the carrot rounds, garlic, bay leaf, and thyme. Scatter the bones around the veal. Place the meat in the oven and bake thirty minutes. Turn the meat, cover loosely with foil, and bake forty-five minutes longer.

4. Turn the meat once more and add the tarragon sprigs to the skillet. Cover loosely with foil and bake forty-five minutes longer.

5. Remove the roast and discard the bones. Add the cream to the skillet and place it on the stove. Stir to dissolve the brown particles that cling to the bottom and sides of the skillet. If dried tarragon is used, add one teaspoon. Simmer five minutes and put the sauce through a fine sieve. If fresh tarragon is available, add it now. Do not add dried tarragon to the sauce after it is put through a sieve. When ready to serve, bring the sauce to the boil and swirl in the remaining butter. Slice the veal and serve with the sauce.

6. Serve with Carrots Vichy (page 218).

Rôti de Veau à l'Estragon

(Veal roast with tarragon)

10 or more servings

1 4-pound rump roast of veal
Salt and freshly ground pepper
    to taste
6 tablespoons butter
1 cup coarsely chopped onion
½ cup coarsely chopped celery
½ cup coarsely chopped carrot
2 whole cloves garlic, crushed
    but unpeeled
4 sprigs fresh thyme or 1 tea-
    spoon dried

1 bay leaf
2 to 4 sprigs fresh tarragon
3 tablespoons flour
2 cups Veal Broth (page 197) or
    chicken broth
1½ cups heavy cream
2 teaspoons chopped fresh tar-
    ragon or 1 teaspoon dried
1 tablespoon Cognac

1. Preheat the oven to 400 degrees.

2. Sprinkle the meat all over with salt and pepper. Place it in a shallow roasting pan and rub with four tablespoons of the butter. Place in the oven and bake one hour.

3. Turn the meat to the other side. Scatter the onion, celery, carrot, garlic, thyme sprigs, and bay leaf around the meat. Strip the leaves from the tarragon stem and save the stem for the sauce. Arrange the tarragon sprigs around the meat.

4. Roast thirty minutes, basting occasionally. Reduce the oven heat to 375 degrees. Cover the roast with foil and continue baking thirty to forty minutes, basting often.

5. Remove the roast from the oven and cover with foil to keep warm. Pour the cooking liquid and vegetables into a casserole or large skillet. Skim off and discard surface fat. Cook the sauce to about half its original volume. Strain the sauce through a fine sieve into a saucepan.

6. As the sauce cooks down, melt two tablespoons of butter in a saucepan and add the flour, stirring with a wire whisk. Add the broth, stirring rapidly. When thickened and smooth, cook about five minutes.

7. Add this sauce to the strained veal sauce in the saucepan. Bring to the boil and add the cream. Cook about five minutes, stirring often. It is not necessary to strain this sauce, but it will be smoother and silkier if it is put through a very fine sieve, preferable the kind known in French as a chinois.

8. Return the sauce to the boil and add the chopped tarragon and Cognac. Serve the meat sliced with the sauce spooned over.

9. Serve with Puréed Potatoes (page 213) and Braised Endives (page 216).

Rôti de Veau au Karvi

(Roast veal with caraway)

6 to 8 servings

1 3½-pound loin of veal
2 cloves garlic, slivered lengthwise
Salt and freshly ground pepper
   to taste

2 teaspoons caraway seeds
1¼ cups water
½ cup coarsely chopped carrot
¾ cup coarsely chopped onion

1. Preheat the oven to 400 degrees.

2. Make incisions between the ribs of the veal and insert slivers of garlic in the incisions. Sprinkle the roast on all sides with salt, pepper, and caraway seeds.

3. Place the veal in a shallow roasting pan and add one-quarter cup of water. Bake thirty minutes and reduce the oven heat to 350 degrees. Turn the roast.

4. Scatter the carrot and onion around the veal and add half a cup of water. Cover with foil and bake forty-five minutes. Add the remaining water. Remove the foil and continue baking about thirty minutes longer. Serve the veal sliced with the pan juices.

5. Serve with Potatoes in Cream Sauce (page 214).

This recipe is from Roger Fessaguet, chef of La Caravelle restaurant in New York.

Quasi de Veau Normande

(Roast rump of veal with Calvados)

8 to 10 servings

3 pounds cracked, chopped veal
   bones
5½ pounds boneless rump of
   veal, tied with string
Salt and freshly ground pepper
   to taste
1 cup chopped onion
1 cup diced carrot
½ cup diced celery

4 cloves garlic, crushed
1 bay leaf
1 sprig fresh thyme or ½ teaspoon dried
5 tablespoons Calvados
1 cup dry white wine
1 pound mushrooms, thinly
   sliced
4 cups heavy cream

1. Preheat the oven to 425 degrees.

2. Arrange the bones in one layer in a baking dish (an oval dish measuring 10 x 16 inches is suitable). Place in the oven and bake forty-five minutes. Stir the bones.

3. Sprinkle the rump of veal with salt and pepper and arrange on the bones. Continue baking forty-five minutes.

4. Remove the roast and keep warm. Scatter the onion, carrot, celery, garlic, bay leaf, and thyme over the bones. Return the rump to the dish, browned side down, on top of the bones. Cover closely with foil and return to the oven.

5. Bake two hours, basting occasionally. Remove the foil and continue cooking, basting often, fifteen minutes. Remove from the oven.

6. Transfer the roast to a warm place and cut away and discard the string. Cover veal with foil until ready to carve.

7. Remove and discard the bones. Place the pan on the stove and reduce the sauce over high heat to about one-third of the original volume. Add four tablespoons of Calvados and the wine. Add the juices that may have accumulated around the roast as it stands.

8. Strain the sauce into a skillet using a fine sieve, preferably the sort known in French as a chinois. Using the back of a wooden spoon, extract as much liquid from the vegetable solids as possible.

9. Add the mushrooms and cook fifteen minutes.

10. Add the cream and cook down over high heat, stirring often from the bottom. Cook about twenty minutes, or until sauce is a bit syrupy. When ready, there should be about five cups of sauce. Add the remaining tablespoon of Calvados.

11. Slice the roast and serve with the hot sauce.

12. Serve with Carrots Vichy (page 218).

Roast Rognonnade of Veal

8 to 12 servings

1 5- to 6-pound boned, ready-to-roast loin of veal with kidney and fillet (see instructions)
Salt and freshly ground pepper to taste
The cracked bones
1 tablespoon peanut, vegetable, or corn oil
½ cup chopped celery with leaves
¾ cup cubed carrots
¾ cup coarsely chopped onion
1½ cups coarsely cubed tomato
2 whole cloves garlic
3 sprigs parsley
1 bay leaf
2 sprigs fresh thyme, or 1 teaspoon dried
½ cup dry white wine
1 cup Veal Broth (page 197) or chicken broth

1. Preheat the oven to 400 degrees.

2. Sprinkle the roast all over with salt and pepper. Arrange the bones over the bottom of a shallow baking dish (an oval dish measuring about

10 x 16 inches is ideal). Add the roast and brush with oil.

3. Bake fifteen minutes and turn the roast over. Roast fifteen minutes longer and scatter around the roast the celery, carrots, onion, tomato, garlic, parsley, bay leaf, and thyme.

4. Bake fifteen minutes longer and add the wine and veal broth. Reduce the oven heat to 375 degrees. Cover the roast loosely with aluminum foil.

5. Continue baking one hour. Turn the roast once more. Do not re-cover but continue baking, basting often, for thirty to forty-five minutes longer. The total baking time is from two hours and fifteen minutes to two and one-half hours.

6. Strain the pan liquid through a sieve, preferably a fine mesh sieve known in French as a chinois. Add the vegetables to the sieve and press to extract as much of their liquid as possible. Discard the vegetables. Put the strained pan liquid in a saucepan and bring to the boil. Reduce for about ten minutes, skimming off the fat as it accumulates. Meanwhile, keep the roast in a warm place loosely covered with foil.

7. Remove the string from the roast and add the sauce to the baking pan, stirring to dissolve the brown particles that cling to the bottom and sides of the pan. Continue cooking in the oven for ten minutes, basting often with the pan liquid.

8. Serve the roast sliced with the hot pan liquid. If you wish a slightly thicker sauce, you may dissolve about one tablespoon cornstarch or arrowroot in cold water and stir it into the boiling sauce.

9. Serve with Purée of Celery Root (page 215).

How to prepare a rognonnade of veal for roasting

1. Carefully cut away the kidney from the loin of veal, cutting through the fat that surrounds it. Cut and pull away the fat around the kidney and discard it. Set the kidney aside.

2. Neatly cut around the fillet of the veal. Cut away and discard any fat around the fillet. Reserve the fillet.

3. Scrape around the two large end bones of the veal loin. Pull up on the bones, then carve around them. Remove and save the bones.

4. Using a boning knife, cut around the rib bones, following the contours of the bones with the knife. Save the bones.

5. Lay the boned meat skinned side down and open it up. Trim off and discard all fat on the exposed meat. Leave a meaty flap attached to the boned loin portion. Slice off the very bottom of the flap. The attached flap should be about eight inches long. The cut-away bottom portion could be used for stews.

6. Split both the fillets and kidneys lengthwise.

7. Sprinkle the opened-up loin and flap with salt and pepper. Arrange the kidneys, ends touching, in a single row atop the loin. Arrange the fillet halves with thick end to thin end next to the kidneys. Sprinkle with salt and pepper. Roll the meat to enclose the kidney and the fillet.

8. Truss and tie the meat in eight places with string. If necessary, use the trimmed-off meat from the flaps to patch exposed places. Tie well.

9. Run the string lengthwise around the roast, looping it over, under and around the eight pieces of trussing string. The roast is now ready to be cooked with the bones.

This recipe is from the Four Seasons in New York.

Kalbsnieren Braten

(Roast loin of veal Swiss-style with kidney)

12 or more servings

1 14-pound whole loin of veal (half a saddle) with bone in	1½ cups chopped onion
1 veal kidney, trimmed of fat and split in half lengthwise	½ teaspoon chopped sage
Salt and freshly ground pepper to taste	1 cup chopped celery
2 bay leaves	¾ cup chopped carrot
3 cloves garlic, unpeeled	1½ cups dry white wine
	1 cup Veal Broth (page 197) or chicken broth

1. Have the butcher bone the loin of veal. Make certain that when it is boned, all the meat and fleshy part of the veal are kept intact. This will include the large loin, the fillet, and the long flap extending from the loin. Have most of the interior fat cut away. Cut away and discard the very tail end of the flap. Or use it for another purpose. The boned loin should measure about 11 x 12 inches. Save the bones and crack them.

2. Preheat the oven to 400 degrees.

3. Lay out the whole boned loin, skin side down. Cut away the fillet and split it in half lengthwise.

4. Arrange the fillet and kidney pieces along the center of the boned loin. Sprinkle all the meat with salt and pepper and roll it. Tie neatly and compactly with string. Sprinkle the outside with salt and pepper.

5. Pour half a cup of water in a shallow roasting pan (one that measures about 12 x 18 inches is suitable). Scatter the bones around the roast.

6. Place the roast in the oven and bake one hour. Turn the roast every fifteen minutes as it cooks.

7. Scatter the bay leaves, garlic, onion, sage, celery, and carrot around the roast. Reduce the oven heat to 350 degrees. Roast thirty minutes longer, turning every ten minutes.

8. Cover with foil and continue roasting and turning as before for thirty minutes. The total cooking time is two hours.

9. Remove the roast and remove the string. Keep the roast warm by covering with foil.

10. Place the roasting pan on the stove and add the wine. Scrape and stir with a wooden spoon to dissolve the brown particles that cling to the bottom and sides of the pan. Return the roast to the pan. Do not cover. Place the pan in the oven and continue roasting, basting often to glaze the veal, fifteen minutes.

11. Remove the pan from the oven and remove the veal. Keep it warm by covering with foil. Strain the pan gravy into a saucepan. Add the veal broth. Cook the sauce down, skimming off and discarding fat as it appears. Reduce the sauce to two cups or slightly less.

12. Slice the roast and serve with the sauce.

13. Serve with Puréed Potatoes (page 213).

Braised Leg of Veal Italian-Style

10 or more servings

1 8- to 10-pound boned, rolled, and tied leg of veal
Salt and freshly ground pepper to taste
¼ cup butter
1 teaspoon finely chopped garlic
1 teaspoon finely chopped rosemary or sage
1½ cups coarsely chopped onion
¾ cup coarsely chopped carrot
¾ cup coarsely chopped celery
Veal Broth (page 197) or chicken broth
1 tablespoon arrowroot or cornstarch
¼ cup dry sherry

1. Preheat the oven to 375 degrees.

2. Sprinkle the meat all over with salt and pepper. Rub it with butter and sprinkle with garlic and rosemary.

3. Scatter the onion, carrot, and celery over the bottom of a baking dish with a lid. Add the meat and cover.

4. Bake until the meat is quite tender, about two hours. If necessary, add a little veal broth to prevent sticking.

5. Remove the meat and strain the pan liquid. If there are not two cups of liquid, add enough veal broth to measure that amount. Put the liquid in a saucepan and bring to the boil.

6. Blend the arrowroot with the sherry and stir it into the sauce. Pour the sauce over the meat and bake about five minutes longer. Serve the meat sliced with the sauce and buttered pasta.

This recipe is from the Café Chauveron, Bay Harbor Island, Florida.

Longe de Veau Farcie

(*Stuffed loin of veal*)

12 or more servings

1 14-pound whole loin of veal (half a saddle)
¼ cup wild rice
½ pound lean veal, cut into small cubes
1¾ cups heavy cream
Salt and freshly ground pepper to taste
2 ounces foie gras, cut into half-inch cubes
2 tablespoons butter at room temperature
1 bay leaf
2 sprigs fresh thyme or 1 teaspoon dried

1 cup chopped onion
1 cup chopped celery
¾ cup chopped carrots
1 cup chopped tomatoes
6 sprigs fresh parsley
1 tablespoon chopped fresh tarragon or 1 teaspoon dried
½ cup Veal Broth (page 197) or chicken broth
1 tablespoon arrowroot or cornstarch
2 tablespoons Cognac

1. Have the butcher bone the loin of veal. Make certain that when it is boned, all the meat and fleshy part of the veal are kept intact. This will include the large loin, the fillet, and a long flap extending from the loin. Have most of the interior fat cut away. Cut away but reserve the tail end from the flap. Save the bones and crack them.

2. Preheat the oven to 400 degrees.

3. Lay out the whole boned loin, skin side down. Cut away the fillet and split it in half lengthwise.

4. Cook the rice in a large quantity of salted water until tender. Drain. There should be about half a cup. Set aside.

5. Add the cubed veal to the container of a food processor or electric blender. If a blender is used, this will have to be done in two or more steps. Add one cup of the cream while processing on high speed. Add salt and pepper to taste. Spoon and scrape this mixture into a mixing bowl. Add the rice and foie gras. Blend well.

6. Spoon the mixture over the loin of veal, concentrating it over the thick part. Arrange the two pieces of fillet over the mixture. Roll the roast.

7. Divide the reserved tail end of the flap in half. Cover each end of the stuffed roast with a piece of the tail end to keep the filling intact. Tie the roast compactly. Sprinkle with salt and pepper.

8. Arrange the roast in a shallow roasting pan (one that measures about 12 x 10 inches is suitable). Smear the top of the roast with butter and place in the oven. Bake fifteen minutes.

9. Scatter the bay leaf, thyme, onion, celery, carrot, tomato, and parsley around the roast. Reduce the oven heat to 350 and continue roasting forty-five minutes. Cover with foil.

10. Continue roasting one hour and fifteen minutes. Remove the foil. Untie the roast and discard the string. Continue roasting about fifteen minutes longer, basting often.

11. Remove the roast and keep warm covered with foil. Spoon and scrape the roasting liquid and vegetables into a saucepan. Add the tarragon and veal broth. Cook down, skimming fat from the surface as necessary.

12. Blend the arrowroot and Cognac and add them to the sauce, stirring. Add the remaining three-fourths cup of cream and simmer about five minutes.

13. Strain the sauce, putting it through a sieve, preferably of the sort known in French kitchens as a chinois. Press the solids with the back of a heavy spoon to extract as much of the juices as possible. Discard the solids. There should be about two cups of sauce.

14. Slice the roast and serve with sauce.

15. Serve with Braised Endives (page 216).

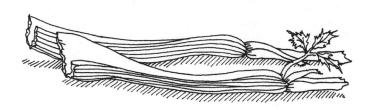

This recipe is from the Quo Vadis restaurant in New York.

Vitello Tonnato
(*Cold veal with tuna mayonnaise*)

8 to 12 servings

3 pounds veal rump in one large
  piece
10 anchovies
6 cups Veal Broth (page 197) or
  chicken broth
1½ cups dry white wine
6 peppercorns
2 cups coarsely chopped onion
1 cup coarsely chopped celery
1 cup chopped leeks (optional)
½ cup coarsely chopped carrot
2 cloves garlic
1 bay leaf

¼ teaspoon thyme
6 sprigs parsley
1 7-ounce can tuna fish packed
  in oil, drained
1½ cups very thick, lightly
  salted Mayonnaise (page 200)
2 tablespoons capers for garnish
4 or more cornichons or other
  pickles, sliced
Quartered hard-cooked eggs
  (optional)
Sprigs of rosemary or parsley

1. If necessary, tie the veal in several places with string to keep it whole. Put in a kettle with cold water to cover and bring to the boil. Drain well.

2. Make numerous gashes with the pointed thin blade of a small knife over the surface of the meat. Cut two or three of the anchovies into four pieces. Insert the pieces into the gashes.

3. Return the meat to a clean kettle and add the broth, wine, peppercorns, onion, celery, leeks, carrot, garlic, bay leaf, thyme, parsley, and remaining anchovies. Do not add salt at this time. Simmer forty-five minutes and turn the meat in the broth. Let the meat cool in the broth.

4. Remove the meat and chill it. If the sauce has jellied, scrape it off the meat and return it to the kettle.

5. Heat the cooking liquid. Strain it into a clean kettle or saucepan, pressing with the back of a heavy spoon to extract the juices. Reduce the cooking liquid to two cups. Let cool. It must be quite cool but not jellied.

6. Put the tuna in the container of a food processor or blender and process to a fine purée. Scrape it into a bowl.

7. Gradually add one cup of the cooking liquid, stirring constantly. Add the mayonnaise, gradually, beating. Gradually beat in the remaining liquid. Stop adding if the sauce becomes too thin. It should be of a consistency to coat the meat when sliced. Taste for seasoning.

8. Cut the meat into very thin slices. Arrange them neatly and symmetrically over a cold serving dish. Spoon the sauce over, reserving about one and one-half cups. Garnish with capers, cornichons, hard-cooked egg wedges, and sprigs of rosemary or parsley.

9. Serve, if desired, with Cold Rice Salad (page 213) and with the additional sauce on the side.

Eggplant with Veal Stuffing

6 to 10 servings

4 tablespoons butter
1½ cups finely chopped onion, about ½ pound
1 clove garlic, finely minced
1 pound fresh mushrooms, finely chopped, about 4 cups
Juice of one lemon
Salt and freshly ground pepper to taste
3 tablespoons chopped parsley
1½ teaspoons finely chopped fresh thyme or ½ teaspoon dried
2 tablespoons finely chopped fresh basil

½ pound cooked veal, finely chopped
10 tablespoons fresh bread crumbs
7 tablespoons freshly grated Parmesan cheese
2 large, or 3 medium, eggplants, about 2½ pounds
Flour for dredging
1 cup peanut, vegetable, or corn oil
Tomato Sauce I (page 203)

1. Heat the butter and add the onion and garlic. Cook, stirring, until onion is wilted, about five minutes. Add the mushrooms, lemon juice, salt, pepper, parsley, thyme, and basil. Cook over relatively high heat, stirring frequently, until liquid has almost completely evaporated, eight to ten minutes.

2. Add the veal and cook, stirring, about four minutes. Add six tablespoons of bread crumbs and three tablespoons grated Parmesan cheese.

3. Trim off the ends of the eggplants and cut each into half-inch slices.

4. Pour the flour onto a baking dish and add salt and pepper to taste. Dredge the eggplant slices in the mixture on both sides, shaking off excess.

5. Heat about one-quarter cup of oil in a large, heavy skillet and add as many eggplant slices as the skillet will hold. Cook until golden brown on one side, one and one-half to two minutes, adding more oil, little by little. The point is to add as much oil as necessary, but as little as possible. Turn the slices, cook until golden on that side and drain on paper towels. Continue adding slices and oil as necessary until the slices have been cooked on both sides.

6. Select a rectangular, square, or oval baking dish. Arrange the smaller slices of eggplant, sides touching, on the bottom of the dish.

Spoon the filling in the center, spreading it out almost, but not quite, to the edges and mounding it in the center. Cover with remaining eggplant, overlapping as necessary.

7. Blend the remaining bread crumbs and cheese and sprinkle over all.

8. When ready to cook, preheat the oven to 400 degrees. Bake thirty-five to forty minutes or longer. Remove the dish and pour off the fat that will have accumulated on top and around the edges. Let cool slightly. Serve with the tomato sauce.

Roast Loin of Veal

8 or more servings

1 5½-pound loin of veal (half a saddle) with bone in
Salt and freshly ground pepper to taste
2 tablespoons butter
½ cup cubed carrot
½ cup cubed celery
½ cup cubed onion
1 small clove garlic
1 cup cubed fresh or canned tomato
6 sprigs fresh parsley
3 sprigs fresh thyme or ½ teaspoon dried
1 bay leaf

1. Preheat the oven to 425 degrees.

2. Sprinkle the loin with salt and pepper and rub it all over with butter.

3. Arrange the loin in a shallow roasting pan, fat side up. Place the pan in the oven and bake thirty minutes, basting occasionally.

4. Turn the meat fat side down and scatter the carrot, celery, onion, and garlic around it. Bake fifteen minutes, basting occasionally.

5. Turn the meat fat side up and scatter the tomato around it. Tie the parsley, thyme, and bay leaf in cheesecloth and add it.

6. Reduce the oven heat to 400 degrees and bake fifteen minutes.

7. Cover the meat with foil and bake about thirty minutes longer. Total baking time is about one and one-half hours. Carve the loin and serve with the pan juices.

8. Serve with Macaroni au Gratin (page 209).

Homemade Manicotti

10 to 12 servings

THE MANICOTTI

1 cup flour   ⅛ teaspoon nutmeg, or to taste
2 eggs   2 tablespoons melted butter
Salt to taste   1¼ cups milk

THE FILLING

1 10-ounce package fresh spin-   ⅛ teaspoon grated nutmeg, or
   ach   to taste
1½ cups chopped cooked veal   Tabasco to taste
2 tablespoons butter   Salt and freshly ground pepper
3 tablespoons flour   to taste
1¼ cups milk

THE PREPARATION

3 cups Tomato Sauce III (page   7 tablespoons butter
   204)   ½ cup grated Parmesan cheese

1. To make the manicotti, place the cup of flour in a mixing bowl and add the eggs, salt, nutmeg, and melted butter. Stir with a wire whisk to blend and gradually add the milk, stirring. Strain the batter.

2. Pour a tablespoon or so of the batter into a lightly greased six- or seven-inch crêpe pan and cook briefly on one side. Turn and cook briefly on the other. Continue making crêpes until all the batter is used. There should be from twenty to twenty-four crêpes.

3. Cook the spinach in a small amount of boiling water and drain. Press to extract most of the moisture. There should be about one cup. Chop it finely and put it in a mixing bowl with the veal.

4. Melt two tablespoons of butter in a saucepan and add the flour. Stir to blend with a wire whisk and gradually add the milk, stirring constantly with the whisk. When the mixture is thickened and smooth, add the nutmeg, Tabasco, salt, and pepper. This sauce is called a béchamel.

5. Add the béchamel to the veal mixture and stir to blend.

6. Lay out the crêpes on a flat surface and spoon equal portions of the veal mixture into the center of each. Roll the crêpes and arrange them in two flat oval or rectangular baking dishes.

7. Heat the tomato sauce and add four tablespoons of butter.

8. Spoon a light layer of tomato sauce over the manicotti. Melt the remaining three tablespoons of butter and pour over all. Sprinkle with cheese. Bake in a 375° oven for fifteen minutes, or until the manicotti are piping hot and bubbling. Run briefly under the broiler and serve hot with additional tomato sauce and grated cheese on the side.

•Chops•

The purest veal has a flavor so delicate it could almost be said to have no flavor at all. That is not true, of course. The meat simply has a purity of flavor unlike any other. Which is probably why it marries well with a multitude of flavors, and this is nowhere better evidenced than in these veal-chop recipes. Consider the following dishes: veal with seafood and asparagus with a béarnaise sauce; veal with woodland mushrooms; veal with sorrel; veal with cucumber.

One of the most celebrated dishes of the past few decades—saddle of veal Orloff—is a highly ambitious and difficult dish to prepare. In fact, it is best made in professional kitchens. In this section, we offer an admirable version of this dish made with a simple veal chop. It contains puréed onions and mushrooms blended in a béchamel sauce and baked with a light cheese topping.

As a final note, a simple sauté of veal chops (and that is the basis for the vast majority of recipes) requires cooking the seasoned chops in butter or other fat for about ten minutes. The chops are turned and cooked ten minutes on the other side. It's as simple as that.

Chops are cut from the rack or loin of veal.

This recipe is from the Elms Inn of Ridgefield, Connecticut.

Côtes de Veau Anna Maria

*(Veal chops with artichokes
and mushrooms)*

4 servings

4 loin veal chops, about
⅟₂ pound each
Salt and freshly ground pepper
to taste
¼ cup flour
3 tablespoons butter
2 teaspoons finely chopped shallots
2 or more large mushrooms cut
into thin julienne strips,
about 1 cup

1 9-ounce package frozen artichoke hearts, broken apart
1 teaspoon crushed green peppercorns, available where imported foods are sold
1 cup dry champagne, or use a
dry, still white wine
1 cup heavy cream

1. Sprinkle the chops with salt and pepper. Dredge lightly on both sides in flour.

2. Melt two tablespoons of butter in a heavy skillet and cook the chops on both sides, browning well, about twenty minutes. Turn the chops once or twice as necessary to brown evenly.

3. Remove the chops to a warm place and cover to keep warm.

4. To the skillet add the remaining butter and shallots. Cook briefly and add the mushrooms and artichoke hearts. Cook, stirring oc-casionally, about five minutes and add the peppercorns. Add the cham-pagne and cook over high heat until the liquid is reduced to about one-third cup. Stir as necessary to dissolve the brown particles that cling to the bottom and sides of the skillet.

5. Add the cream and cook over high heat about five minutes. Add salt and pepper to taste. Pour the sauce with the vegetables over the chops and serve.

6. Serve with Grilled Tomatoes with Oregano (page 217).

This recipe is from Mario's restaurant in the Bronx, New York. It is that of the Migliucci family.

Costoletti di Vitello con Peperonni Sott'aceto

(Veal chops with basil, peppers, and vinegar)

6 servings

6 loin veal chops, about
¾ pound each
Salt and freshly ground pepper
to taste
Flour for dredging
1 cup olive oil
6 cloves garlic, crushed and
peeled
1 cup Veal Broth (page 197) or
chicken broth

6 torn or coarsely chopped fresh
basil leaves or 1 teaspoon
dried
3 cups sweet red peppers
packed in vinegar, the peppers cut into ½-inch strips
¾ cup red wine vinegar
2 tablespoons chopped parsley

1. Sprinkle the chops with salt and pepper. Coat well with flour and shake off the excess.

2. Heat half the oil in a large skillet and cook the chops on both sides until nicely browned, about twenty minutes.

3. Pour off the fat and clean the skillet. Add the remaining oil and the garlic. Cook about five minutes and add the chops. Add the broth. Sprinkle the chops with basil and pepper strips. Add the vinegar, salt, and pepper. Cook ten to fifteen minutes. Sprinkle the parsley over all and serve.

4. Serve with Puréed Potatoes (page 213).

This recipe is from the Petite Marmite restaurant in Palm Beach, Florida.

Veal Chops Petite Marmite

(Breaded stuffed veal chops)

4 servings

4 loin veal chops, about ½
pound each
4 thin slices prosciutto or boiled
ham
12 thin slices black truffles
Salt and freshly ground pepper
to taste
2 eggs

Flour for dredging
1½ cups fine bread crumbs
½ cup freshly grated Parmesan
cheese
4 tablespoons peanut, vegetable,
or corn oil
2 tablespoons butter

1. Butterfly the chops. That is to say, slice them horizontally through the center to the bone. Open up the chops and place them split side up on a flat surface. Pound each wing flap lightly with a flat mallet.

2. Arrange one slice of prosciutto (it should be trimmed to fit neatly) over one flap of each chop. Arrange three slices of truffle, edges overlapping, down the center of each ham slice. Fold the second wing flap over. Sprinkle both sides of the chops with salt and pepper.

3. Beat the eggs in a flat dish and set aside.

4. Dredge the chops on both sides in flour and shake off the excess. Dip in the egg to coat on both sides.

5. Blend the crumbs and grated cheese and dredge the chops on both sides in this, tapping the sides to help the coating adhere.

6. Heat the oil and butter in a heavy skillet and cook the chops until golden brown on both sides, about ten minutes to a side.

7. Serve with Creamed Spinach (page 218).

Veal à la Oskar was, according to legend, named for King Oskar of Sweden. The story goes that he admired the young beauties of his country and would secretly take them to midnight suppers at one small hideaway or another in Stockholm. He was particularly fond of veal, asparagus, and crawfish, and the chef of one restaurant had the inspiration to combine the ingredients in one preparation. It was thus named veal à la Oskar.

As time has passed, many kinds of seafood have been substituted for the crawfish, which have a short season and even then are difficult to obtain. Both crabmeat and shrimp are excellent substitutes.

Veal à la Oskar

*(Veal with asparagus, seafood,
and béarnaise sauce)*

4 servings

4 loin veal chops, about ½ pound each
Salt and freshly ground pepper
8 asparagus spears
2 tablespoons plus 1 teaspoon butter
¼ pound lump crabmeat or 4 cooked, peeled shrimp
¾ cup Béarnaise Sauce (page 198)

1. Sprinkle the chops on both sides with salt and pepper to taste. Skewer the tail of each chop to hold it neatly in place. Set aside.

2. Scrape the sides of the asparagus spears but leave the tips intact. Put in a skillet with cold water to cover and salt to taste. Bring to the boil and simmer about three minutes, or until crisp-tender. Drain.

3. Heat two tablespoons of butter in a heavy skillet large enough to hold the chops in one layer. Brown the chops on one side, about ten minutes. Turn and brown the other, about ten minutes.

4. Melt a teaspoon of butter in a small skillet and add the crabmeat or shrimp. Cook briefly just to heat through.

5. As the chops cook, prepare the béarnaise.

6. Arrange the chops on a serving platter and garnish each with two asparagus spears. Spoon béarnaise sauce over the asparagus and garnish the top of each serving with crabmeat or shrimp. Serve immediately with Baked Rice (page 211).

This is a recipe of Paul's Landmark restaurant in New York.

Veal Chops with Sweetbread Stuffing

4 servings

4 veal chops, butchered of all but the main rib bone
1 pair Sweetbreads Braised with Port (see following recipe)
½ cup liquid from braised sweetbreads
4 tablespoons butter
3 tablespoons finely chopped shallots
½ cup finely chopped mushrooms

2 tablespoons finely chopped parsley
Salt and freshly ground pepper to taste
Flour for dredging
2 tablespoons peanut, vegetable, or corn oil
¼ cup port
½ cup Veal Broth (page 197) or chicken broth

1. Butterfly the chops or have them butterflied by the butcher. That is to say, split them down the center to the rib bone. Open them up and pound lightly with a flat mallet. Take care not to break the flesh.

2. Prepare the sweetbreads and let them cool. Set aside the strained cooking liquid. Cut the sweetbreads into small cubes and set aside.

3. Heat one tablespoon of butter in a skillet and add the shallots. Cook, stirring, until wilted and add the mushrooms. Cook, stirring, about five minutes and add the chopped sweetbreads, stirring to blend. Add the parsley and three tablespoons of the braising liquid from the sweetbreads. Blend and let cool.

4. Preheat the oven to 400 degrees.

5. Open up the veal chops and sprinkle with salt and pepper. Dredge lightly on both sides in flour.

6. Heat the oil and one tablespoon of butter in a heavy skillet large enough to hold the opened-up chops in one layer. Add the chops and cook until golden brown, one or two minutes to a side.

7. Grease a baking dish with one tablespoon of butter. Arrange the opened-up chops in the dish and spoon equal parts of the sweetbreads over each chop.

8. Place in the oven and bake just to heat thoroughly.

9. Pour off the fat from the skillet and dab with paper towels to remove excess fat, leaving the brown solids that cling to the pan.

10. Heat the pan and add the wine, reserved liquid from the braised sweetbreads, and broth. Stir to dissolve the brown particles that cling to the bottom and sides of the pan. Swirl in the remaining tablespoon of butter and strain the sauce over the chops.

11. Serve with Braised Endives (page 216).

Sweetbreads Braised with Port

1 pair sweetbreads, about 1 pound
1 strip bacon, cut into thin strips
1 tablespoon butter
1 onion, peeled and thinly sliced, about ½ cup
1 small carrot, thinly sliced, about ½ cup
1 small celery rib, sliced cross- wise, about ½ cup
1 bay leaf
1 clove garlic, peeled and left whole
¼ teaspoon thyme
¼ cup port
½ cup Demi-glace (page 197) or canned beef gravy

1. Prepare the sweetbreads according to the instructions on page 155. The weighting-down part of the process is essential.

2. Preheat the oven to 400 degrees.

3. Cook the bacon in a skillet until rendered of fat and add butter. Add the onion, carrot, celery, bay leaf, garlic, and thyme. Stir.

4. Add the sweetbreads, wine, and demi-glace and place in the oven. Do not cover. Cook, basting often, about thirty minutes. Strain the liquid and reserve. There should be about half a cup.

5. Use for stuffing veal chops in preceding recipe.

Côtes de Veau Fermière

(Baked veal chops with potatoes and onions)

6 servings

6 loin veal chops, about ½
  pound each
Salt and freshly ground pepper
  to taste
2 or 3 potatoes, about 2 pounds
1 or 2 onions, about ½ pound

2 tablespoons butter
1 clove garlic, crushed
1 cup Veal Broth (page 197) or
  chicken broth
1 teaspoon dried thyme
1 bay leaf

1. Preheat the oven to 350 degrees.

2. Trim off most of the fat from the chops. Pound each chop well with a flat mallet and sprinkle with salt and pepper.

3. Peel the potatoes and cut them into thin slices, about one-eighth inch thick. There should be four or five cups. Drop the slices immediately into cold water to cover so they will not discolor.

4. Cut the onions in half and slice them as thinly as possible. There should be two or three cups. Set aside.

5. Heat the butter in a heavy skillet and brown the chops lightly on one side. Do not cook through. Turn and cook lightly on the other side.

6. Scatter the onions over the chops and add the garlic to the center. Drain the potatoes well and scatter them over all. Sprinkle with salt and pepper. Pour the veal broth over all and add the thyme and bay leaf. Cover with a piece of wax paper cut to fit.

7. Bring to the boil on top of the stove and place the skillet in the oven. Bake about fifteen minutes and discard the wax paper. Cook, basting often, fifty minutes to one hour, or until the chops are fork tender. Run the skillet under the broiler to brown.

8. Serve with Carrots Vichy (page 218).

French chefs have a passion for giving poetic names to their creations. Belles des bois, or "beauties of the woods," refers in this case to the woodland mushrooms known as morels. Morels can at times be found fresh in wooded areas. They can also be found in cans or dried in specialty shops. They are expensive and are, therefore, for celebration dishes such as this.

This recipe is from Le Cirque restaurant in New York.

Côtes de Veau Belles des Bois

(Veal chops with morels)

6 servings

⅓ ounce dried morels, available in fine food stores
6 loin veal chops, about ½ pound each
Salt and freshly ground pepper
14 tablespoons butter
2 tablespoons finely chopped shallots
Juice of half a lemon
6 tablespoons dry white wine
1 cup heavy cream
1 tablespoon Madeira or dry sherry
¼ cup flour
1 cup Veal Broth (page 197) or chicken broth

1. Place the morels in a mixing bowl and add hot (not boiling) water to cover. Let stand until cool. Drain well and pat dry.

2. Sprinkle chops with salt and pepper and set aside.

3. Heat four tablespoons of the butter in a skillet and add the shallots. Cook briefly, stirring, and add the morels. Cook, shaking the skillet, about three minutes. Add the lemon juice, cover and cook about five minutes. Add two tablespoons white wine, cover, and simmer five minutes. Add the cream, cover, and cook over relatively high heat about fifteen minutes. At this point the cream should be fairly well reduced and thickened. Add salt and pepper to taste and the Madeira. Swirl two tablespoons of butter into the sauce.

4. Dredge the chops in flour. Heat the remaining eight tablespoons of butter in a large skillet and add the chops. Cook over high heat about five minutes, or until nicely browned on one side. Turn and cook about fifteen minutes on the other side. Do not overcook or the chops will dry out.

5. Remove the chops to a warm serving platter. Pour off most of the fat from the skillet. Add the remaining four tablespoons of white wine and cook briefly. Add the veal broth and cook over relatively high heat until reduced to about one-quarter cup. Return the chops to the skillet. Spoon and scrape the mushrooms over all. Stir.

6. Serve the chops with the mushrooms in sauce spooned over.

7. Serve with Buttered Fine Noodles (page 209).

Côtes de Veau à l'Estragon

(*Veal chops with tarragon*)

8 servings

8 loin veal chops, about ½ pound each
Salt and freshly ground pepper to taste
½ cup flour
11 tablespoons butter
4 fresh tarragon stems or 1 teaspoon dried
½ pound thinly sliced mushrooms, about 4 cups

2 tablespoons finely chopped shallots
½ cup dry white wine
1 tablespoon chopped fresh tarragon or 1 teaspoon dried
1 cup Veal Broth (page 197) or chicken broth

1. Sprinkle the chops on both sides with salt and pepper. Dredge on all sides in flour.

2. Heat eight tablespoons of butter in a large skillet and, when it is hot, add the chops. Cook about five minutes on one side until nicely browned. Add the tarragon stems and turn the chops. Cook the chops for about twenty minutes in all.

3. Remove the chops and keep warm. Add the mushrooms to the skillet. Add the shallots, salt, pepper, and wine, stirring. Add the tablespoon of chopped fresh tarragon. Cook until wine is reduced by half. Add the broth and cook over high heat, stirring often, about five minutes.

4. Swirl in the remaining butter. Add the chops and baste briefly with the sauce. Serve hot.

5. Serve with Potatoes in Cream Sauce (page 214).

One of the commonest names on French menus is <u>grandmère</u>, or "in the style of grandmother." It really means a form of elegant but nostalgic cooking, and the ingredients include salt pork, onions, and potatoes.

Côtes de Veau Grandmère

(Veal chops with potatoes and onions)

4 servings

4 loin veal chops, about ½ pound each

Salt and freshly ground pepper to taste

¾ pound potatoes, cut into sticks about the shape of thick French-fried potatoes, about 1½ cups

4 small white onions, less than ¼ pound, peeled

¼ pound salt pork, cut into small "batons," or sticks

5 tablespoons butter

½ cup dry white wine

½ cup Veal Broth (page 197) or chicken broth

2 tablespoons finely chopped parsley

1. Sprinkle the chops on both sides with salt and pepper and set aside.

2. In a saucepan combine the potatoes and onions. Add cold water to cover. Bring to the boil and simmer about two minutes. Drain well.

3. In another saucepan, combine the salt pork and water to cover. Bring to the boil. Drain well. Cook the salt pork in the saucepan until it is rendered of fat. Add one tablespoon of the butter. Add the four onions and cover. Cook six to eight minutes. Uncover and brown the onions slightly.

4. Using a slotted spoon, remove the salt pork, leaving the onions in the pan. Add the potatoes and cook about five minutes, turning the pieces often until golden brown. Drain.

5. Add two tablespoons of butter to the pan. Return the onions, potatoes, and salt pork to the pan.

6. Meanwhile, heat two tablespoons of butter in a very heavy skillet and add the chops. Cook to brown on one side, about seven minutes. Turn and cook on the other side about fifteen minutes. When ready, the chops should be uniformly brown. Remove the chops and cover with foil to keep warm.

7. To the skillet, add the wine and cook down until almost totally reduced. Add the broth and simmer about two minutes. Strain the sauce over the chops and scatter the potatoes and onions and salt pork over all. Sprinkle with chopped parsley.

8. Serve with Creamed Spinach (page 218).

Côtes de Veau Bonne Femme

(Veal chops with potatoes, onions, and mushrooms)

To the preceding recipe, add ½ pound mushrooms, sliced or quartered, with the potatoes in Step 4.

Breaded Veal Chops

6 servings

6 loin veal chops, about
  ½ pound each
½ cup flour
1 egg
1 tablespoon water
Salt and freshly ground pepper
  to taste

5 tablespoons plus 1 teaspoon
  peanut, vegetable, or corn oil
1 cup fine fresh bread crumbs
3 tablespoons butter

1. Trim off almost all the fat from each chop. Pound the chops well with a flat mallet and dredge lightly in flour.

2. Combine the egg, water, salt, and pepper and one teaspoon of oil in a flat dish. Dip the veal chops in the mixture and then in bread crumbs to coat both sides. Pat down lightly with the flat side of a heavy knife to help the crumbs adhere.

3. Heat the remaining oil in a skillet large enough to hold the chops and add one tablespoon of butter. When very hot, add the chops and cook over moderately low heat about eight minutes. Turn and continue cooking about fifteen minutes. Transfer to hot plates. Pour off the fat from the skillet and add the remaining butter. Cook until hazelnut brown and pour over the chops.

4. Serve with Asparagus Milanaise (page 219).

The origin of certain dish names is frequently obscure. Andrea Doria was an admiral in the Italian navy. The name Doria on menus, however, invariably indicates the presence of cucumbers in one form or another.

This recipe is from Doros restaurant in San Francisco.

Côtes de Veau Andrea Doria

(Stuffed veal chops with rosemary and vegetables)

4 servings

4 loin veal chops, about ½ pound each
4 thin slices prosciutto or other ham
4 thin slices Fontina, Gruyère, or Swiss cheese
4 thin slices black truffle (optional)
Salt and freshly ground pepper to taste
2 tablespoons plus 1 teaspoon butter
4 "new" red potatoes, peeled
4 solid rectangles of cucumber, peeled and seeds removed, each measuring about 1 x 2 inches
1 tablespoon peanut, vegetable, or corn oil
4 large mushroom caps
1 tablespoon finely chopped shallots
2 tablespoons finely chopped onion
1 tablespoon finely chopped rosemary
¼ cup dry vermouth
½ cup Demi-glace (page 197) or canned beef gravy
4 red, ripe cherry tomatoes, stems removed

1. Preheat the oven to 400 degrees.

2. Cut a pocket in the loin side of each chop for stuffing. Insert one slice each of prosciutto, cheese, and truffle. Secure with wooden skewers or toothpicks.

3. Sprinkle the chops with salt and pepper.

4. Heat two tablespoons of butter in a large heavy skillet and add the chops. Cook, turning as necessary, until nicely browned.

5. Meanwhile, place the potatoes, water to cover, and salt to taste in a saucepan and bring to the boil. Simmer three minutes and add the cucumber pieces. Cook two minutes longer. Drain.

6. Heat the oil and one teaspoon butter in a skillet and add the potatoes. Cook five minutes until they are golden. Add the mushroom caps and cook about ten minutes, turning the pieces as necessary.

7. When the chops have been browned for ten minutes, place them in the oven. Sprinkle with the chopped shallots, onion, and rosemary. Bake ten minutes. Transfer the chops to a warm serving platter.

8. To the skillet in which the chops cooked add the vermouth, stirring to dissolve the brown particles that cling to the bottom and sides of the pan. Add the demi-glace and heat thoroughly.

9. Add the cherry tomatoes and blanched cucumber pieces to the potatoes and mushrooms, shaking the skillet to heat the vegetables evenly. Cook until piping hot throughout.

10. Top each chop with a mushroom cap. Scatter the remaining vegetables over the meat. Spoon the pan sauce over all and serve.

This recipe is from Windows on the World in New York.

Windows Veal Chops

4 servings

4 center-cut loin veal chops, about ½ pound each
Salt and freshly ground pepper to taste
3 cups heavy cream
2 ribs celery, trimmed
6 green onions, trimmed
1 carrot, trimmed and scraped

¼ pound mushrooms
¼ cup chopped parsley
2 teaspoons peanut, vegetable, or corn oil
1 tablespoon drained green peppercorns
¼ cup Cognac

1. Preheat the oven to 350 degrees.

2. Sprinkle the chops on both sides with salt and pepper.

3. Pour the cream into a saucepan and cook over high heat until reduced to one and one-half cups.

4. Cut the celery into two-inch lengths. Cut the pieces into very thin slices and cut the slices into very thin julienne strips. There should be about one cup, loosely packed.

5. Cut the green onions into two-inch lengths. Cut the pieces into very thin julienne strips. There should be about three-quarters of a cup, loosely packed.

6. Cut the carrot into very thin slices. Cut the slices into very thin julienne strips. There should be about two cups, loosely packed.

7. Thinly slice the mushrooms. There should be about two cups.

8. Combine all the shredded vegetables, mushrooms, and parsley. Add salt and pepper and toss to blend.

9. Heat the oil in a very heavy skillet and, when hot, add the chops. Cook five minutes, turning once.

10. Butter a baking dish large enough to hold the chops in one layer and arrange the chops in the dish. Scatter the vegetable mixture over the chops.

11. Sprinkle the green peppercorns over the vegetables. Blend the Cognac and cream. Pour the cream mixture over all and bake twenty minutes.

12. Serve with Baked Rice (page 211).

This recipe is from the Mills Hyatt House in Charleston, South Carolina.

Veal Chops with Creamed Mushrooms

4 servings

THE CHOPS

4 loin veal chops, about ½ pound each
Salt and freshly ground pepper to taste

2 tablespoons flour
2 tablespoons peanut, vegetable, or corn oil
3 tablespoons butter

THE CREAMED MUSHROOMS

¼ pound mushrooms
3 tablespoons plus 1 teaspoon butter
1 tablespoon finely chopped shallots

Salt and freshly ground pepper to taste
½ cup heavy cream
1 teaspoon flour

THE HAM AND CHEESE

4 thin slices prosciutto or boiled ham

4 thin slices Gruyère or Swiss cheese

1. Sprinkle the chops with salt and pepper. Dust on both sides with flour and shake off the excess.

2. Heat two tablespoons of oil and one tablespoon of butter in a large heavy skillet and add the chops. Cook seven or eight minutes. Turn the chops and cook five minutes longer.

3. Pour off the fat from the skillet. Add two tablespoons of butter to the skillet and continue cooking the chops over low heat about ten minutes.

4. Meanwhile, thinly slice the mushrooms. There should be about two cups.

5. Melt three tablespoons of butter in a saucepan and add the shallots. Cook briefly, stirring, and add the mushrooms. Sprinkle with salt and pepper. Add the cream and stir, simmering about one minute.

6. Blend the remaining teaspoon of butter with the flour and add it to the creamed mushrooms, stirring. Cook briefly until thickened.

7. Heat the prosciutto briefly under the broiler.

8. Arrange the chops on a baking dish and top each chop with a slice of prosciutto. Spoon equal portions of the creamed mushrooms on each serving. Cover with a slice of cheese. Run briefly under the broiler until the cheese melts.

9. Serve with Grilled Tomatoes with Oregano (page 217).

This recipe is from Chez la Mère Blanc in Vonnas, France.

Côtes de Veau à l'Oseille

(Veal chops with sorrel sauce)

4 servings

4 loin veal chops, about ½ pound each
Salt and freshly ground pepper to taste
½ pound fresh sorrel leaves
4 tablespoons butter
½ cup onions cut into small uniform dice
½ cup carrots cut into small uniform dice
½ cup dry white wine
½ cup heavy cream
Juice of half a lemon

1. Sprinkle the chops with salt and pepper and set aside.

2. Rinse and drain the sorrel and pat or shake dry. Tear off and discard any tough stems. Set the sorrel aside.

3. Heat the butter in a skillet large enough to hold the chops in one layer. Add the chops and cook about ten minutes until nicely browned. Turn and cook ten minutes to brown the other side.

4. Sprinkle the onions and carrots around and between the chops. Cook three minutes. Remove the chops.

5. Add the wine and cook down until the sauce is a bit syrupy. Add the cream and cook over high heat about three minutes until slightly thickened.

6. Pour the sauce and vegetables through a fine sieve of the sort the French call a chinois. Or purée them in a food mill. Return the sauce to the skillet.

7. Shred the sorrel leaves finely and add them to the sauce. Immediately add the juice of half a lemon. Heat thoroughly at a slow simmer.

8. Serve the hot sauce over the chops.

9. Serve with Baked Rice (page 211).

Some sources attribute the name Orloff to one Count Grigou Orlov who lived in Russia in the eighteenth century. Others state that the name is simply that of a noble family that held sway in Moscow during the reign of Nicholas the Great from 1826 to 1855.

The most famous dish that bears the name Orloff is <u>selle de veau</u>, or saddle of veal, Orloff. During the days of the czars, French, not Russian, was the language used by the aristocrats. Many of the nobles imported French chefs to staff their kitchens. French chefs today are modestly agreed that all of the best dishes that bear Russian names are of French origin.

The recipe below is made with veal chops and is an adaptation of the saddle of veal Orloff.

Côtes de Veau Orloff

(Glazed veal chops with puréed onions and mushrooms)

6 servings

6 loin veal chops, about ½ pound each
Salt and freshly ground pepper to taste
1 pound white onions
10 tablespoons butter
¼ pound mushrooms
4 tablespoons flour

2 cups milk
¼ teaspoon nutmeg
⅛ teaspoon cayenne pepper
⅓ cup heavy cream
2 egg yolks
⅓ cup grated Parmesan cheese
½ cup Veal Broth (page 197) or chicken broth

1. Sprinkle the chops with salt and pepper and set aside.

2. Peel the onions and cut them in half. Cut the halves into very thin slices.

3. Heat four tablespoons of butter in a saucepan and add the onions. Sprinkle with salt and pepper and cook slowly, stirring frequently, about ten minutes.

4. Rinse, drain, and thinly slice the mushrooms and add them to the onions. Cover and cook about ten minutes, stirring occasionally.

5. As the onions cook, make a béchamel or white sauce. Heat three tablespoons of butter in a saucepan and add the flour, stirring with a wire whisk. When blended and smooth, add the milk, stirring rapidly with the whisk. When thickened and smooth, continue cooking, stirring occasionally around the bottom. Add nutmeg, cayenne, and salt and pepper to taste. Cook about ten minutes in all.

6. Stir about three-quarters cup of the béchamel sauce into the onion-and-mushroom mixture. Set the remaining sauce aside.

7. Spoon the onion-and-mushroom mixture into the container of an electric blender or food processor. Blend, stirring down as necessary. When well blended, transfer the mixture to a saucepan and cook, stirring frequently, about thirty-five minutes.

8. Preheat the oven to 400 degrees.

9. Heat three tablespoons of butter in a large, heavy skillet and add the chops. Cook on one side until golden brown, about five minutes. Continue cooking and turning the chops about twenty minutes.

10. As the chops cook, bring the reserved béchamel sauce to the boil. Add heavy cream and remove the sauce from the heat. Add the egg yolks and half the Parmesan. The sauce with the cheese is now called a mornay. Bring the sauce just to the boil, stirring rapidly, and remove it from the heat.

11. Spoon a thin layer of the onion-and-mushroom mixture over the bottom of a baking dish (an oval dish that measures about 10 x 16 inches is ideal).

12. Arrange the chops over the onion-and-mushroom mixture and spoon equal parts of the remaining mixture over each chop. Spoon equal parts of the mornay sauce over each chop. Sprinkle the chops with the remaining Parmesan cheese. Add the veal broth. Place the dish in the oven and bake thirty minutes.

13. Serve with Braised Fennel (page 216).

•Scaloppine•

In compiling this book of recipes, a hundred or more well-known restaurants were requested to contribute some of their most favored veal recipes. It came as no surprise that the vast majority of them replied with recipes for dishes made with veal scaloppine. The reasons why are almost too obvious to elaborate on.

What can you say about veal scaloppine except that there is no limit, other than one's own imagination, to the uses to which this cut of meat can be put? Scaloppine can be sautéed, of course. They can be cut into small cubes, cut into thin strips, rolled and stuffed with an endless variety of fillings, smothered, or layered and baked.

And you could fill a dictionary of cooking with the assortment of flavors that can be used to alter, in the finest sense, the nature of veal scaloppine.

Scaloppine are thin slices of meat taken from the leg or loin. As cut in this country, however, they are sometimes one-quarter inch thick or more and are referred to as cutlets. (Similarly, small, thin veal steaks are also referred to as cutlets.)

Generally speaking, scaloppine are pounded, preferably with a flat mallet, before cooking. This hastens the cooking time. Some chefs and cooks recommend pounding the veal with a "claw mallet." We disagree. We think this abuses the meat and gives it a poor texture.

The scaloppine recipes range from the grillades of Louisiana to a marvelous *saltimbocca alla romana* from the chef of a small Italian restaurant in Amagansett, Long Island. One of the finest recipes is the scaloppine of veal with morels, sent to us by the proprietor of the distinguished Chez Bardet restaurant in Montreal.

One of the most valuable sets of recipes in this section may be a sequence on how to bread veal scaloppine, plus variations from a French kitchen.

Escalopes de Veau aux Herbes

4 servings

12 slices veal (scaloppine), about 1 pound
2 tablespoons peanut, vegetable, or corn oil
¼ teaspoon crumbled sage, chopped
¼ teaspoon rosemary leaves, chopped
Salt and freshly ground pepper to taste
5 tablespoons butter
1 clove garlic, finely minced
1 tablespoon parsley
1 dried hot red pepper, crumbled, or ½ teaspoon dried pepper flakes
Juice of half a lemon

1. Flatten the scaloppine lightly with a flat mallet.

2. Blend the oil, sage, rosemary, salt, and pepper and spoon the mixture over the veal, making certain that the veal is gently coated. Cover and let stand one hour.

3. Heat two tablespoons of butter in a large, heavy skillet and add half the meat in one layer. Cook about two minutes to a side and turn. Cook quickly, about two minutes on the other side, and transfer to a hot platter. Cook remaining meat in the same way without adding more butter.

4. To the skillet, add two tablespoons of butter and the garlic, parsley, and hot pepper. Add one more tablespoon of butter, the juice of half a lemon, and salt to taste. Cook briefly and pour the sauce over the meat.

5. Serve immediately with Baked Rice (page 211).

This recipe is from Tony's restaurant in Houston.

Tony's Veal Riccadonna
(*Veal with vermouth*)

4 servings

16 slices veal (scaloppine), about 1¼ pounds
2 tablespoons flour
Salt and freshly ground pepper to taste
2 tablespoons olive oil
2 tablespoons butter
1 tablespoon finely chopped shallots
¼ cup sweet vermouth
¼ cup dry vermouth
2 tablespoons finely chopped parsley
½ teaspoon oregano

1. Place the scaloppine on a flat surface and pound lightly with a flat mallet.

2. Blend the flour with salt and pepper and dredge the meat on both sides.

37

3. Heat the oil and butter in one large or two smaller skillets and add the shallots. Cook briefly, stirring. Add the meat and brown quickly on both sides, about one minute to a side. If two skillets are used, combine the ingredients of both skillets in one.

4. Blend the sweet and dry vermouths and add to the skillet, turning the meat in the sauce while cooking briefly. Sprinkle the parsley and oregano over the meat, turning.

5. Serve with Baked Rice (page 211).

This dish gets its name from the fact that one of its ingredients is green peppercorns, which are grown in Malagasy, otherwise known as Madagascar. This is the recipe of Trader Vic's in San Francisco.

Veal Malagasy

(Veal with mushrooms in a cream sauce)

4 servings

8 to 12 slices veal (scaloppine), about 1 pound
Salt and freshly ground pepper to taste
2 tablespoons flour
3 tablespoons butter
¼ cup finely chopped onion
¼ pound thinly sliced mushrooms

1 teaspoon crushed green peppercorns, available where fine imported foods are sold
¼ cup dry white wine
½ cup heavy cream
½ teaspoon Worcestershire sauce
Juice of half a lemon

1. Pound the pieces of meat lightly with a flat mallet. Sprinkle them with salt and pepper and dust with flour. Shake off excess.

2. Heat the butter in a large, heavy skillet. When hot but not browning, add the meat. Cook over high heat about one and one-half minutes to each side.

3. Remove the meat. To the skillet, add the onion, mushrooms, and peppercorns. Cook briefly and add the wine. Cook quickly to reduce and add the cream. Bring to the boil. Stir in the Worcestershire sauce and lemon juice. Add salt to taste. Return the meat to the skillet and heat through.

4. Serve with Buttered Fine Noodles (page 209).

This recipe is from Brennan's restaurant in Houston.

Veal Béarnaise

4 servings

1 pound veal, cut into very thin
  julienne strips
Salt and freshly ground pepper
  to taste
Dash of cayenne pepper
¼ teaspoon ground cumin

¼ teaspoon paprika
1½ teaspoons finely chopped
  garlic
2 tablespoons butter
¾ cup Béarnaise Sauce (page
  198)

1. Toss the veal with salt, pepper, cayenne, cumin, paprika, and garlic.

2. Heat the butter in a large heavy skillet and, when it is very hot, add the veal. Cook over high heat, tossing and stirring, until veal is lightly browned and cooked. This must be done hastily or the veal will dry out.

3. Serve the veal on four individual beds of rice that has been tossed with chopped parsley. Spoon béarnaise sauce over each serving.

Our introduction to Montreal restaurants was a dinner at Chez Bardet, after which we decided it is one of the great French restaurants on the North American continent. This is the dish on which we dined.

Escalopes de Veau aux Morilles

*(Veal scallops with
morels in cream sauce)*

4 servings

1 cup canned morels or ⅓ ounce
  dried (see note)
4 slices veal (scaloppine), about
  1 pound
Salt and freshly ground pepper
  to taste

2 tablespoons flour
3 tablespoons butter
1 tablespoon finely chopped
  shallots
½ cup dry sherry
1 cup heavy cream

1. Soak the morels well in advance if dried morels are used. Set aside. Otherwise drain the canned morels and set aside.

2. Pound the veal lightly with a flat mallet.

3. Sprinkle the veal with salt and pepper. Dredge lightly in flour and shake off excess.

4. Heat the butter in a heavy skillet and add the veal. Cook five to six minutes, turning once to brown well on both sides.

5. Remove the veal to a warm platter. Add the shallots to the skillet. Cook briefly and add the sherry. Cook, stirring, until it is almost evaporated. Add the cream and salt and pepper to taste. Add the drained morels and heat through.

6. Pour the sauce over the veal and serve immediately.

7. Serve with Baked Rice (page 211) and Braised Fennel (page 216).

NOTE: Canned morels are available in specialty shops that deal in fine imported foods. Dried morels are also available and quite costly. Remember that it takes only a third of an ounce of dried morels to make this dish. The dried mushrooms should be soaked in hot water until they expand. They may contain a good deal of sand, which will appear in the soaking liquid. Carefully pour off the liquid and discard the sandy portion. This recipe may also be made with one cup of sliced fresh ordinary mushrooms that have been cooked in a tablespoon of butter.

There are as many Bolognese recipes in Italy as there are cooks. Here are two versions.

Scaloppine di Vitello Bolognese I

(Breaded scaloppine with prosciutto, cheese, and truffles)

4 servings

4 slices veal (scaloppine), about ¼ pound each
Salt and freshly ground pepper to taste
¼ cup flour
1 egg
2 tablespoons water
2 cups fresh bread crumbs
¾ cup grated Parmesan cheese
4 tablespoons peanut, vegetable, or corn oil

1 tablespoon butter
4 thin slices prosciutto or other ham
4 to 8 slices Fontina or Gruyère cheese, about ⅓ pound total weight
8 thin slices white truffles, available where fine imported Italian foods are sold

1. Pound the veal pieces lightly with a flat mallet. Sprinkle the meat with salt and pepper to taste. Dredge the pieces all over in flour.

2. Beat the egg with the water in a flat dish and add salt and pepper to taste. Coat the meat on all sides in egg, patting with the fingers.

3. Dip the meat in bread crumbs blended with Parmesan cheese to coat on all sides. Tap the sides lightly with the flat side of a heavy knife to help the crumbs adhere.

4. Heat the oil and butter in one or two skillets and add the meat. Cook until golden brown on one side, about three minutes. Turn. Arrange the prosciutto neatly on top of each scaloppine. Cover the ham with the cheese. Top each serving with two truffle slices. Cover the veal closely and let cook three to five minutes, or until veal is cooked through and cheese is hot and melted.

5. Serve with Risotto (page 212).

Scaloppine di Vitello Bolognese II

4 servings

4 slices veal (scaloppine), about ¼ pound each
Salt and freshly ground pepper
Flour for dredging
2 tablespoons butter

2 tablespoons olive oil
6 tablespoons Marsala
4 very thin slices prosciutto
4 thin slices Gruyère or Swiss cheese

1. Pound the meat lightly with a flat mallet but without breaking the fibers. Sprinkle on both sides with salt and pepper and dredge all over in a little flour.

2. Heat the butter and oil in a heavy skillet large enough to hold the meat in one layer. When it is very hot, add the meat. Brown quickly on both sides and transfer to a hot baking pan large enough to hold the pieces in one layer. Keep warm.

3. Add the Marsala to the skillet and cook, stirring, over high heat until the wine becomes syrupy. Spoon this over the scaloppine. Top each piece of meat with one slice of prosciutto and with a slice of cheese and run quickly under the broiler until the cheese melts.

4. Serve with Risotto (page 212).

This recipe is from Perditas restaurant in Charleston, South Carolina.

Veal Scallops Isobel

4 servings

8 thin slices veal (scaloppine),
　about 1½ pounds
1 cup drained tomatoes
2 tablespoons tomato paste
1 teaspoon sugar
Salt and freshly ground pepper
　to taste
½ cup water
1 tablespoon freshly grated Par-
　mesan cheese

2 tablespoons olive oil
1 teaspoon chopped garlic
½ teaspoon oregano
¼ teaspoon thyme
½ cup dry red wine
2 tablespoons flour
1 tablespoon butter
8 thin slices mozzarella cheese
Chopped parsley for garnish
8 thin slices lemon for garnish

1. Pound the veal lightly with a flat mallet and set aside.

2. In the container of a food processor or blender, combine the tomatoes, tomato paste, sugar, salt, pepper, water, and Parmesan cheese. Blend well.

3. Heat half the oil in a small saucepan and add the garlic, oregano, and thyme. Cook briefly and add the red wine. Bring to the boil and reduce the wine by half. Combine with the tomato mixture.

4. Sprinkle the veal with salt and pepper and dredge in flour.

5. Heat the remaining oil and the butter in a large skillet and brown the veal on both sides, about two or three minutes. Remove veal to a warm place. Pour off the fat from the skillet.

6. Add the tomato mixture to the skillet and stir. Return the veal and cook, stirring to coat. Simmer ten minutes.

7. Top each piece of veal with a slice of mozzarella cheese. Run under the broiler until cheese melts. Garnish with chopped parsley and lemon slices.

8. Serve with spaghetti, fettuccine, or other pasta. Braised Celery (page 217) would also serve well as a vegetable.

This recipe is from Jasper's Italian Restaurant in Kansas City, Missouri.

Lemon Veal with Eggplant

4 servings

8 slices veal (scaloppine), about 1½ pounds
Salt and freshly ground pepper to taste
½ pound eggplant, peeled and cut into 8 ¼-inch-thick rounds
Flour for dredging

2 eggs, lightly beaten
1 cup fine fresh bread crumbs
½ cup plus 3 tablespoons peanut, vegetable, or corn oil
1 tablespoon butter
8 thin, seeded lemon slices
1 teaspoon oregano
1 tablespoon chopped parsley

1. Pound the meat lightly with a flat mallet and sprinkle with salt and pepper.

2. Sprinkle the eggplant rounds with salt and pepper. Dredge in flour and shake off the excess. Dip in egg, then in bread crumbs. Pat to help the crumbs adhere.

3. Heat the half cup of oil and cook the eggplant pieces on both sides until golden. Drain on paper towels.

4. Dip the pieces of veal in flour and shake off excess. Dip in egg to coat each piece well.

5. Heat the three tablespoons of oil and the butter in a skillet and cook the veal, two or three pieces at a time, until golden. Turn and cook on the other side. Continue until all the meat is cooked.

6. Arrange the veal on a platter, slices slightly overlapping. Top each slice with an eggplant round and lemon slice. Sprinkle with oregano and parsley and serve hot.

7. Serve with a tossed green salad.

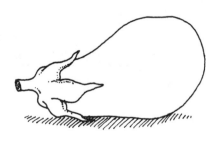

This recipe is from Giannino's restaurant in Milan.

Veal with Tomatoes and Peas

4 servings

8 slices veal (scaloppine), about
  1½ pounds
Salt and freshly ground pepper
  to taste
2 tablespoons flour
1 cup fresh or frozen very young
  peas
3 tablespoons butter

2 tablespoons olive oil
1 teaspoon chopped sage leaves
½ cup dry white wine
¾ cup drained tomatoes,
  puréed in a blender or food
  processor
½ cup Veal Broth (page 197) or
  chicken broth

1. Pound the scaloppine lightly with a flat mallet. Sprinkle the meat with salt and pepper and dredge on both sides in flour.

2. Put the peas in a small heavy saucepan with a tight-fitting lid. Add one tablespoon of butter and cook over low heat until done.

3. Meanwhile, heat two tablespoons of butter and two tablespoons of oil in a large, heavy skillet and add the meat, turning the pieces as necessary to brown lightly on both sides. Cook over high heat, about two minutes to a side.

4. Sprinkle the meat with sage. Add the wine, tomatoes, and veal broth. Cook, turning the slices of meat in the sauce and shaking the skillet. Cook the sauce down to a consistency that coats the meat. Add the cooked peas and stir to blend them into the sauce.

5. Serve with Polenta (page 215).

This recipe is from the Tack Room of the Rancho del Rio Resort and Tennis Club of Tucson, Arizona.

Tack Room Veal with Pfifferlinge Mushrooms

4 servings

8 slices veal (scaloppine), about
  1 pound
Salt and freshly ground pepper
  to taste
2 tablespoons flour
5 tablespoons butter
1 7-ounce can imported Pfif-

ferlinge mushrooms, available where fine imported
  foods are sold
½ cup dry sherry
2 tablespoons finely chopped
  parsley

1. Pound the veal slices with a flat mallet. Sprinkle with salt and pepper and dredge lightly in flour. Shake off the excess.

2. Heat three tablespoons of butter in a heavy skillet and add the veal. Cook five to six minutes, turning once to brown well on both sides.

3. Remove the veal to a warm platter. Add the remaining butter to the skillet and cook, stirring, until it is the color of hazelnuts. Do not burn. Add the drained mushrooms. Add the sherry and ignite it.

4. Pour the mushrooms and sauce over the veal. Sprinkle with parsley.

5. Serve with Baked Rice (page 211).

This recipe is from the Pfister Hotel and Tower in Milwaukee, Wisconsin.

Veal Scaloppine with Ham, Mushrooms, and Tomatoes on Spaghetti

4 servings

8 thin slices veal (scaloppine), about 1½ pounds
Salt and freshly ground pepper to taste
1 tablespoon butter
1 tablespoon peanut, vegetable, or corn oil
1 tablespoon finely chopped shallots
1 clove garlic, finely minced
¼ pound mushrooms, thinly sliced

¾ cup dry white wine
⅓ pound prosciutto, cut into thin julienne strips
¾ cup diced, drained, canned peeled tomatoes
1 cup Demi-glace (place 197) or canned beef gravy
2 teaspoons arrowroot
2 tablespoons dry red wine
1 pound spaghetti, cooked according to package directions, tossed in butter and parsley

1. Pound the meat lightly with a flat mallet. Sprinkle with salt and pepper.

2. Heat the butter and oil in a skillet and add the meat. Cook quickly until browned on one side. Turn and cook until browned on the other, about four minutes in all.

3. Remove the meat and add the shallots and garlic. Cook briefly and add the mushrooms. Cook until wilted. Add the white wine and cook until most of the liquid evaporates. Add the prosciutto and stir.

4. Add the tomatoes and demi-glace. Cook down over high heat, about five minutes.

5. Blend the arrowroot and red wine. Stir it into the sauce and bring to the boil. Return the meat to the sauce and baste briefly.

6. Serve the meat with buttered spaghetti tossed with parsley.

This recipe is from La Grange Restaurant in Los Angeles.

Escalopes de Veau Arboisienne

(Veal scaloppine with mushrooms and onions)

4 servings

12 slices veal (scaloppine), about
  1½ pounds
Salt and freshly ground pepper
  to taste
2 tablespoons flour
16 very small white onions,
  peeled
3 tablespoons butter
1 cup whole button mushrooms
1 7-ounce can imported wild

mushrooms, such as Pfif-
  ferlinge, available where fine
  imported foods are sold
1 tablespoon finely chopped
  shallots
¾ cup dry white wine
½ cup Demi-glace (page 197) or
  canned beef gravy
3 tablespoons finely chopped
  parsley

1. Pound the scaloppine with a flat mallet and sprinkle with salt and pepper. Dredge in flour and shake off excess.

2. Put the onions in a small saucepan and add water to cover and salt to taste. Bring to the boil and simmer eight to ten minutes.

3. Heat the butter in a large, heavy skillet and, when hot, cook the scaloppine until golden on one side, about two minutes. Turn and cook until golden on the other side, about two minutes. Remove the meat and keep warm in a serving dish.

4. Add the drained mushrooms and onions to the skillet. Cook briefly, shaking the skillet. Add the shallots and cook, stirring, about three minutes.

5. Add the wine and cook down over high heat about four minutes. Add the demi-glace and cook five minutes longer. Pour the boiling sauce over the meat. Sprinkle with chopped parsley.

6. Serve with Carrots Vichy (page 218) and Skillet Potatoes (page 214).

This recipe is from Trader Vic's in San Francisco.

Veal with Morels

4 servings

1 cup canned morels, or ⅓
    ounce dried (see note)
⅓ cup morel liquid
8 slices veal (scaloppine), about
    1½ pounds
Salt and freshly ground pepper
    to taste
Flour for dredging

4 tablespoons butter
¼ cup finely chopped onion
½ cup heavy cream
½ cup milk
1 tablespoon flour
1 teaspoon lemon juice
⅛ teaspoon cayenne pepper

1. Soak the morels well in advance if dried morels are used. Set aside. Otherwise, drain the canned morels and save one-third cup liquid.

2. Pound the veal lightly with a flat mallet. Sprinkle with salt and pepper and dredge lightly in flour. Shake off the excess.

3. Heat three tablespoons of butter in a heavy skillet and add the veal pieces. Cook five to six minutes, turning once to brown well on both sides.

4. Remove the veal to a warm platter. Add the onion to the skillet and cook briefly. Add the morels and one-third cup morel liquid. Cook until the liquid is reduced by half.

5. Add the cream and milk and bring to the simmer. Blend one tablespoon of butter and the flour well and add gradually, stirring into the liquid. When thickened and smooth, add salt and pepper, lemon juice, and cayenne. Pour the sauce over the veal.

6. Serve with Buttered Fine Noodles (page 209).

NOTE: Canned morels are available in specialty shops that deal in fine imported foods. Dried morels are also available and quite costly. But remember that it takes only a third of an ounce of dried morels to make this dish. The dried mushrooms should be soaked in hot water until they expand. They may contain a good deal of sand, which will appear in the soaking liquid. Carefully pour off the liquid and discard the sandy portion. This recipe may also be made with one cup of sliced fresh ordinary mushrooms that have been cooked in a tablespoon of butter.

Saltimbocca is a somewhat whimsically named dish—the exact translation is "jump in the mouth." No one can offer a satisfactory explanation of how it got its name, but it is one of the best-known and best-tasting veal dishes in Italian cookery. This recipe is from the Casa Albona in Amagansett, Long Island.

Eduardo Giurici's
Saltimbocca alla Romana
(Veal with prosciutto and hard-cooked eggs)

2 to 4 servings

6 slices veal (scaloppine), about ½ pound
Salt and freshly ground pepper to taste
Flour for dredging
2 tablespoons olive oil
6 tablespoons butter
2 peeled hard-cooked eggs, each cut in half lengthwise
¾ cup Marsala or medium-dry sherry

¼ teaspoon monosodium glutamate, optional
Escarole or spinach with garlic and oil (see recipe)
6 thin slices prosciutto at room temperature
2 teaspoons finely chopped parsley

1. Pound the veal slices lightly with a flat mallet. Sprinkle with salt and pepper and dredge in flour. Shake off the excess.

2. Heat the oil in a heavy skillet and add the veal. Cook about one minute to a side or until lightly browned. Do not overcook.

3. Transfer the veal to another skillet large enough to hold the meat and egg halves in one layer. Scatter the butter around and over the veal and eggs. Add the Marsala and bring to the boil. Sprinkle with salt, pepper, and monosodium glutamate.

4. Cover the skillet and cook about five minutes, shaking the skillet occasionally so that the ingredients mingle. Uncover and cook about two minutes more, or until the sauce has a slightly thickened consistency.

5. Spoon the escarole or spinach down the center of a serving dish and arrange the veal topped with prosciutto slightly overlapping over the vegetable. Top four of the pieces with egg halves, cut side down. Spoon the sauce over all and sprinkle with parsley.

6. Serve with a tossed green salad.

NOTE: A fresh sage leaf may be added to the veal before the prosciutto.

Escarole (or Spinach) with Garlic and Oil

4 servings

1½ to 2 pounds fresh escarole or spinach, washed well
Salt to taste
2 tablespoons olive oil
4 cloves garlic, each cut into 6 slices

Freshly ground pepper to taste
⅛ teaspoon monosodium glutamate (optional)

1. If escarole is used, pull the leaves apart and trim the ends.

2. Drop the escarole or spinach into boiling water with salt to taste. Bring to the boil and simmer until tender. The escarole will take several minutes, the spinach only a few seconds. Drain.

3. Squeeze the vegetable to extract most of the excess liquid. The vegetable may be prepared in advance to this point.

4. When ready to serve, heat the oil and add the pieces of garlic. Cook just until garlic starts to take on color. Add the vegetable, pepper, and monosodium glutamate and cook, stirring as necessary, so that the vegetable is heated through. Take out and discard the garlic pieces.

Fortified wines team well with many sautéed veal dishes. One of these is Marsala. The dish is quickly made and has just a trace of sweetness from the wine.
This recipe is from the Aperitivo restaurant in New York.

Veal alla Marsala

4 to 6 servings

16 small slices veal (scaloppine), about 1¼ pounds
Salt and freshly ground pepper to taste
Flour for dredging
4 tablespoons peanut, vegetable, or corn oil

5 tablespoons butter
¼ cup Marsala
3 tablespoons Veal Broth (page 197) or chicken broth
1 tablespoon finely chopped parsley

1. Pound the pieces of veal lightly with a flat mallet, taking care not to break the meat. Sprinkle with salt and pepper and dredge lightly in flour.

2. Heat half the oil and, when it is quite hot, add a few pieces of veal, enough to cover the skillet in one layer. Cook rapidly, about one minute

to a side. The meat should be lightly browned. Transfer to a warm platter and add more oil to the skillet. Continue cooking until all the pieces are used.

3. Pour off the fat from the skillet and add four tablespoons of the butter. Return the meat to the skillet and add the Marsala. Cook, stirring to coat the veal, about one minute. Add the veal broth. Cook over high heat briefly. Sprinkle with parsley and swirl in the remaining butter.

4. Serve with Spaghetti with Marinara Sauce (page 210).

Sorrel, which is sometimes called sour grass and is the basis for the French soup called germiny and the Jewish soup called Schav, has been a traditional accompaniment for veal in classic French kitchens since before the time of Escoffier. This recipe is adapted from one by that great master and legendary chef.

Escalopes de Veau à l'Oseille

(Veal scallops in sorrel sauce)

4 to 6 servings

12 slices veal (scalloppine), about 1¼ pounds
½ pound sorrel
4 tablespoons butter
Salt and freshly ground pepper to taste

1 tablespoon finely chopped shallots
¼ cup dry white wine
1 cup heavy cream

1. Pound the veal lightly with a flat mallet.

2. Wash the sorrel leaves well. Discard any tough stems and blemished leaves. Pat dry or use a spin-dryer. Place the sorrel on a flat surface and shred it with a sharp knife. There should be about six cups, loosely packed.

3. Heat one tablespoon of butter and add the sorrel. Add salt and pepper to taste. Cook until sorrel is wilted and remove from the heat.

4. Heat three tablespoons of butter in one or two heavy skillets large enough to hold the scaloppine in one layer. When it is hot, add the scaloppine and cook briefly over moderately high heat until golden brown on both sides. Cook about two minutes to a side. Transfer the meat to a warm platter.

5. Add to the skillet the shallots and the wine. Cook until wine is almost totally reduced. Add the cream and, when it boils, stir in the sorrel. Add salt and pepper and cook about three minutes. Add the veal pieces to the sauce.

6. Serve immediately with Buttered Fine Noodles (page 209).

This is by far the most Southern of all veal dishes. It had its origins in the Cajun country of Louisiana and was for generations served for plantation breakfasts, inevitably accompanied by grits. It makes a fine dish for Sunday brunch as well as for a family supper.

Grillades

(A braised meat dish from Louisiana)

4 servings

8 slices veal (scaloppine), about 1 pound
1 tablespoon finely minced garlic
Salt and freshly ground pepper to taste
¼ teaspoon or more crushed red pepper flakes

Flour for dredging
2 tablespoons oil
1 cup finely chopped onion
1 cup canned tomatoes packed with tomato paste
1 cup water

1. Pound the scaloppine lightly with a flat mallet. Combine the garlic, salt, and pepper and smear this on the meat on both sides. Sprinkle with the pepper flakes and pat them in. Dredge on both sides in flour.

2. Heat the oil in a large, heavy skillet and cook the meat over fairly high heat until golden brown on all sides, about five minutes. Scatter the onion over and around the meat. Cook briefly to wilt and add the tomatoes blended with the tomato paste. Add the water, salt, and pepper. Cover closely and simmer thirty minutes.

3. Serve with buttered grits, cooked according to package directions.

Veal Scallops with Mustard Sauce

3 or 4 servings

8 thin slices veal (scaloppine), about ¾ pound
Salt and freshly ground pepper
⅓ cup flour
4 tablespoons butter
2 tablespoons finely minced shallots

¼ cup dry white wine
½ cup heavy cream
1 tablespoon imported prepared mustard, preferably Dijon or Düsseldorf

1. Place the scaloppine on a flat surface and pound thin with a flat mallet.

2. Sprinkle with salt and pepper and dredge the scaloppine with flour on both sides.

3. Heat the butter in a large, heavy skillet until it is quite hot but not brown. Add the scaloppine and cook quickly until golden, about two minutes on one side, and turn. Cook until golden on the other side. Remove the scaloppine to a warm dish and cover with foil.

4. Add the shallots to the skillet and cook briefly, stirring. Add the wine and cook, stirring, until it is almost totally evaporated.

5. Add the cream and let it boil up, stirring. Cook about thirty seconds and turn off the heat. Stir in the mustard. Do not cook further. Spoon sauce over the meat.

6. Serve with Buttered Fine Noodles (page 209).

This recipe is from Mario's restaurant in Dallas.

Veal with Melon, Mushrooms, and Capers

4 servings

8 thin slices veal (scaloppine), about 1½ pounds	9 tablespoons butter
Salt and freshly ground pepper to taste	8 thin slices of firm, but ripe and sweet, honeydew melon
¼ cup flour	1 egg
½ pound fresh mushrooms, thinly sliced	2 tablespoons milk
	2 teaspoons lemon juice
	½ cup drained capers

1. Pound the scaloppine using a flat mallet. Sprinkle with salt and pepper, dredge in flour, and set aside.

2. Cook the mushrooms in a skillet in two tablespoons of butter until golden brown. Set aside.

3. Slice the melon and have it ready to cook.

4. Beat the egg with milk and add salt and pepper to taste. Dip the veal slices in egg to coat on both sides.

5. Heat six tablespoons of butter in a very heavy skillet and add the coated veal. Cook one and one-half to two minutes on one side. Turn and cook on the second side until golden brown. Remove the veal.

6. Meanwhile, heat one tablespoon butter in a skillet and add the honeydew slices. Cook over high heat about two minutes, turning once. Arrange the slices over the pieces of veal.

7. To the skillet in which the veal cooked, add the lemon juice, mushrooms, and capers, shaking the skillet. Pour this over the veal and serve hot.

8. Serve with Buttered Fine Noodles (page 209).

Charcoal-Grilled Scaloppine with Chive Butter

4 servings

12 thin slices veal (scaloppine), about 1 pound

¼ cup peanut, vegetable, or corn oil

Salt and freshly ground pepper to taste

Chive Butter (page 202)

1. Preheat a charcoal grill until it is quite hot. The coals should be placed quite close to the grill for this recipe, because the meat is only seared on both sides before serving.

2. Brush the veal on both sides with oil and sprinkle with salt and pepper.

3. Prepare the chive butter and have it hot.

4. Put the scaloppine on the grill and cook quickly on both sides, about one minute to a side. Transfer to a hot platter and pour the chive butter over them.

5. Serve piping hot with Grilled Tomatoes with Oregano (page 217) or Carrots Vichy (page 218) and Baked Rice (page 211).

This recipe is from Avon Old Farms Inn, Avon, Connecticut.

Veal Sentino

(Veal with asparagus and cheese)

4 servings

8 asparagus spears

4 slices veal (scaloppine), about ¾ pound

Salt and freshly ground pepper to taste

¼ cup flour

7 tablespoons butter

¼ pound sliced mushrooms, about 2 cups

4 thin slices Fontina or Swiss cheese

Juice of 1 lemon

1. Scrape the sides of the asparagus with a swivel-blade vegetable peeler but leave about two inches of the tips unscraped. Drop the spears into a skillet containing boiling water with salt to taste. Cook two to three minutes until crisp-tender. Do not overcook. Drain.

2. Meanwhile, pound the veal slices lightly with a flat mallet.

3. Sprinkle the veal with salt and pepper and dredge in flour.

4. Heat two tablespoons of the butter in a large, heavy skillet and add the veal. Cook until golden brown, about two minutes to a side.

5. Heat one tablespoon of butter in a skillet and add the mushrooms. Sprinkle with salt and pepper and cook until wilted. Continue cooking until golden brown, stirring as necessary.

6. Preheat the broiler.

7. Arrange the veal slices in one layer on a baking dish. Sprinkle with mushrooms. Arrange two asparagus spears on top of each slice of veal. Cover with the cheese slices. Run under the broiler until cheese melts.

8. Melt four tablespoons of butter and add the lemon juice. Pour the sauce over the veal.

9. Serve with Buttered Fine Noodles (page 209).

No one knows precisely why this simple and delectable dish is called <u>alla Francese,</u> or in the French style. Perhaps, of course, it originated with some French chef who worked in an Italian kitchen many decades ago.

Scaloppine di Vitello alla Francese

(Batter-fried veal with lemon)

4 servings

8 thin slices veal (scaloppine),
  about 1½ pounds
Salt and freshly ground pepper
  to taste
¼ cup flour
1 egg

2 tablespoons milk
6 tablespoons butter
Juice of 1 lemon
8 thin, seeded lemon slices
1 tablespoon finely chopped
  parsley

1. Pound the scaloppine until very thin with a flat mallet. Sprinkle with salt and pepper and dredge on both sides in flour.

2. Beat the egg well and add the milk, salt, and pepper. Blend. Dip the veal in egg to coat on both sides.

3. Heat the butter in a very heavy skillet and add the veal. Cook about two minutes on one side, or until golden. Turn and cook on the second side until golden. Remove the veal and add the lemon juice to the skillet. Pour this over the veal.

4. Garnish with lemon slices and sprinkle with parsley.

5. Serve with Spaghetti with Marinara Sauce (page 210).

This recipe is from the Commander's Palace in New Orleans.

Veal Marcelle

(A version of veal à la Oskar)

4 servings

8 slices veal (scaloppine), about
 1½ pounds
Salt and freshly ground pepper
 to taste
3 tablespoons flour
1 egg
¼ cup milk
3 tablespoons peanut, vegetable,
 or corn oil
3 tablespoons butter
1½ cups thinly sliced
 mushrooms

½ cup chopped green onions,
 green part only
½ pound lump crabmeat
8 cooked asparagus spears, preferably white asparagus,
 heated
1 cup Hollandaise Sauce (page
 199)
½ teaspoon Worcestershire
 sauce

1. Pound the meat lightly with a flat mallet. Sprinkle the meat with salt and pepper and dredge in flour. Shake off excess.

2. Beat the egg with the milk. Dip the veal in the egg mixture until well coated.

3. Heat the oil and one tablespoon of butter in a skillet and cook the veal, two or three pieces at a time, until golden. Turn and cook on the other side. Continue until all the meat is cooked.

4. Heat two more tablespoons of butter in another skillet and add the mushrooms. Cook until wilted and add the green onions. Stir to blend. Add the crabmeat and cook, stirring gently, to heat through.

5. Arrange two slices of the veal on each of four warm serving plates. Spoon equal portions of the crab mixture over the veal. Garnish with two asparagus spears. To the hollandaise, add the Worcestershire sauce and spoon it over each serving.

6. Serve with Carrots Vichy (page 218).

This recipe is from the Aperitivo restaurant in New York.

Piccata di Vitello

(Veal with lemon)

4 servings

8 thin slices veal (scaloppine), about 1½ pounds
Salt and freshly ground pepper to taste
2 tablespoons flour
¼ cup olive oil

4 tablespoons butter
⅓ cup dry white wine
½ cup Veal Broth (page 197) or chicken broth
Juice of 1 lemon
2 tablespoons chopped parsley

1. Pound the veal slices with a flat mallet. Sprinkle with salt and pepper and dredge all over in flour.

2. Heat the oil in a large, heavy skillet and, when it is quite hot, add as many pieces of veal as the skillet will hold in one layer. Cook over high heat to brown on one side, about two minutes. Turn and brown on the other. As the veal is cooked, transfer it to a hot platter.

3. Pour off the fat from the pan and return the pan to the stove.

4. Add the butter and, when it is melted, return the slices to the pan. Cook them on both sides, turning in the hot butter. Add any liquid that may have accumulated on the platter. Add the wine, broth, lemon juice, and parsley. Cook, turning the pieces in the skillet so that they cook evenly, until the sauce has a nice consistency.

5. Serve with Grilled Tomatoes with Oregano (page 217).

Gourmandines de Veau au Gratin S.S. France

(Crêpes stuffed with veal and mushrooms)

8 servings

8 slices veal (scaloppine), about 1½ pounds
16 crêpes (see recipe)
1 pound mushrooms
¼ cup heavy cream
Salt and freshly ground pepper

¼ teaspoon grated nutmeg
6 tablespoons butter plus enough to grease dish
4 cups Mornay Sauce (page 201)
3 tablespoons freshly grated Parmesan cheese

1. Place the scaloppine on a flat surface and pound lightly with a flat mallet. Cut each slice in half.

2. Prepare the crêpes and set aside.

3. Chop the mushrooms finely and put them in a saucepan or deep skillet. Cook, stirring frequently, without adding any fat. Cook about fifteen minutes. Add the cream, salt and pepper to taste, and nutmeg. Continue cooking, stirring frequently, about five minutes longer.

4. Preheat the oven to 450 degrees.

5. Sprinkle the veal pieces with salt and pepper.

6. Heat four tablespoons of butter in a skillet and cook the veal quickly, about thirty seconds on each side, without browning. Transfer the meat to a flat surface and spread each piece with a tablespoon or so of the mushroom purée. Roll each piece jellyroll fashion and wrap each roll with a crêpe.

7. Butter a baking dish lightly and spoon a little mornay sauce over the bottom. Arrange the stuffed crêpes over the bottom and spoon the remaining sauce over all. Sprinkle with grated Parmesan cheese and pour two tablespoons of melted butter over all. Bake twenty-five to thirty minutes. Run the dish under the broiler briefly and serve immediately.

Crêpes

16 to 20 crêpes

1 cup flour	1 tablespoon melted butter plus
2 eggs	enough butter to grease the
Salt	pan
1½ cups milk	

1. Place the flour in a bowl and make a well in the center. Add the eggs, stirring with a wire whisk. Add salt to taste. Beat in half a cup of milk to make a smooth batter. Gradually beat in the remaining milk. Stir in one tablespoon melted butter and put the mixture through a fine sieve.

2. Rub the bottom of a seven-inch crêpe pan with a piece of paper towel that has been dipped in melted butter. Spoon enough of the batter into the pan to barely cover the bottom. Quickly swirl the batter this way and that until the bottom is evenly coated. Cook briefly until the crêpe "sets" and starts to brown on the bottom. Using a spatula, turn the crêpe and cook briefly on the other side without browning. Turn onto wax paper. Continue making crêpes until all the batter is used.

This recipe is from the Troisgros restaurant in Roanne, France.

Escalopes de Veau à la Moutarde

(Veal scaloppine with mustard and mustard seeds)

4 servings

8 to 10 thin slices veal (scaloppine), about 1 pound
Salt and freshly ground pepper
2 teaspoons imported mustard
such as Dijon or Dusseldorf

1 tablespoon mustard seeds
2 tablespoons butter
1¾ cups fresh tomato sauce (see
following recipe)

1. Pound the scaloppine lightly with a flat mallet. Sprinkle on both sides with salt and pepper.

2. Spread half the mustard on one side of the scaloppine. Sprinkle with half the mustard seeds. Turn the scaloppine and spread with remaining mustard and sprinkle with remaining mustard seeds.

3. Heat the butter in a skillet and, when very hot but not burning, add the veal pieces. Cook over very high heat to brown lightly on one side, about thirty seconds. Turn the pieces and cook for about thirty seconds on the other side.

4. Spoon equal portions of the sauce onto each of four hot plates. (Any extra sauce can be refrigerated for future use.) Arrange two or three pieces of veal neatly over the sauce and serve hot.

Fresh Tomato Sauce

1¾ cups

3 red, ripe, unblemished fresh
tomatoes (about ¾ pound)
2 tablespoons butter
2 tablespoons finely chopped
onion

¼ bay leaf
¼ teaspoon thyme
Salt and freshly ground pepper
to taste
1 tablespoon chopped fresh basil

1. Peel the tomatoes and cut away the cores. Chop the tomatoes. There should be about two cups.

2. Heat half the butter in a small skillet and add the onion. When wilted, add the tomatoes, bay leaf, thyme, salt, and pepper. Cook about fifteen minutes.

3. Pour the sauce into the container of a food processor, removing bay leaf, and blend. Return to the skillet. Reheat and swirl in the remaining butter. Put through a fine sieve if desired. Stir in the basil.

Years ago, the late Paula Peck was celebrated for, among a few thousand other good things, her veal rollatine. It is an excellent buffet dish when served cold. In fact, she preferred it that way. If served hot, it may be served with tomato sauce.

Paula Peck's Veal Rollatine

6 or more servings

¾ pound veal, cut into four thin slices of approximately the same size
½ pound Italian sausage in a casing
¼ pound thinly sliced prosciutto
¼ pound thinly sliced Genoa-style salami
1½ cups fine fresh bread crumbs
½ cup finely chopped parsley
½ cup freshly grated Parmesan cheese
Freshly ground pepper to taste
6 tablespoons olive oil
6 large eggs
Salt to taste
7 slices lean bacon
Tomato Sauce III (page 204) (optional)

1. Preheat the oven to 375 degrees.

2. Arrange two large sheets of plastic wrap with edges overlapping on a flat surface.

3. Arrange the slices of veal, edges overlapping, so that you have a large rectangle of meat. Cover with more plastic wrap and pound the meat with a flat mallet until quite thin, without breaking the meat. Remove the top sheet of plastic wrap.

4. Broil the sausage or fry it in a skillet, turning as necessary until done. Drain well.

5. Arrange the slices of prosciutto over the veal, leaving a small margin all around. Overlap the slices. Similarly, make a layer of salami over the prosciutto.

6. In a mixing bowl, combine the bread crumbs, parsley, cheese, and pepper. Add four tablespoons of oil and blend with the fingers. Spoon and smooth this all over the layer of salami.

7. Heat the remaining two tablespoons of oil in a skillet. Beat the eggs well and add them to the skillet. Add salt to taste. Cook, stirring well, until the soft-scrambled stage.

8. Spoon the hot scrambled eggs over the bottom third of the crumbs over the shorter width of the rectangle.

9. Arrange the cooked sausage across the center of the eggs.

10. Start rolling the rectangle, beginning with the egg end. Lift up the plastic wrap as you work to facilitate rolling. When completely rolled, discard the plastic wrap. Cover the meat roll lengthwise with bacon. Tie the meat securely in three or four places with string.

11. Arrange the roll on a rack fitted inside a shallow baking pan. Place in the oven and bake forty-five minutes. Reduce oven heat to 350 and continue cooking fifteen to thirty minutes longer.

12. Serve hot, sliced, with tomato sauce. Or let cool, refrigerate, and serve cold with Cold Rice Salad (page 213).

This is a recipe served to us a short while ago in the Italian villa of Jo and Angelo Bettoja, about an hour's drive from Rome. To prepare it, slices of veal are stacked pancake-fashion with thin slices of mortadella and prosciutto. The meat slices are bound together when baked with a coating of egg. It is served sliced as an appetizer.

Carne Mosaico

(A layered prosciutto and scaloppine loaf)

12 or more servings

8 slices veal (scaloppine), about 1 pound
8 large or 10 medium eggs
½ cup freshly grated Parmesan cheese

Freshly ground pepper to taste
½ pound thinly sliced mortadella
½ pound thinly sliced prosciutto

1. Preheat the oven to 350 degrees.

2. Pound the veal slices with a flat mallet until quite thin. Set aside.

3. Butter a dish to hold the meat in layers. It may be round like a small cake tin, square, or rectangular like a standard loaf pan. It will be necessary to trim and cut the meat to size as the pieces are layered.

4. Beat the eggs with Parmesan cheese and pepper. Do not add salt.

5. Commence making layers starting with veal, continuing with the mortadella, prosciutto, more veal and so on, ending with a layer of veal. Dip each layer of meat in the beaten egg mixture and place it flat in the mold. Continue as indicated. Pour any leftover egg mixture on top. Cover the mold with aluminum foil.

6. Set the mold in a baking dish and pour boiling water around it. Bring to the boil on top of the stove. Place in the oven and bake two hours.

7. Remove and uncover. Place a flat object on top of the meat to weight the meat down. Let stand overnight. To unmold, run a knife between the loaf and the pan; dip bottom of pan into hot water briefly. Trim off and discard ends of loaf. Cut into thin slices and serve as an appetizer.

This is the recipe of Tavern on the Green in New York.

Paupiettes de Veau Gabrielle

(Veal roulades with eggs and cornichons)

4 servings

8 slices veal (scaloppine), about
   1½ pounds
Salt and freshly ground pepper
   to taste
3 large eggs
¼ cup heavy cream

4 tablespoons butter
8 cornichons (imported small,
   sour gherkins) or 4 gherkins
½ cup dry white wine
1 cup heavy cream

1. Pound the scaloppine with a flat mallet. Sprinkle with salt and pepper.

2. Beat the eggs with ¼ cup cream, salt, and pepper. Heat one tablespoon of the butter and add the eggs, stirring gently. Cook until soft-scrambled.

3. Spoon equal amounts of the egg into the center of each scaloppina. Partly sink one cornichon in the center of each batch of egg. Roll the scaloppina to enclose the filling. Tie with string. Sprinkle the outside with salt and pepper.

4. Heat three tablespoons of butter in a heavy skillet and add the veal rolls. Cook to brown nicely all over, about ten minutes, turning often. Remove the meat and keep warm.

5. Add the wine and stir to dissolve the brown particles that cling to the bottom and sides of the pan. Add 1 cup cream and bring to the boil. Add salt and pepper and cook down to a saucelike consistency, about three minutes. Strain the sauce over the veal.

6. Serve with Buttered Fine Noodles (page 209).

Breaded veal dishes have many virtues. First and foremost, they can be delectable. There is a bonus in the fact that the breading "stretches" the amount of meat to be served.

Among the breaded dishes that follow is one of the best known—wiener schnitzel. Schnitzel simply means a veal cutlet or scaloppina, and actually a schnitzel varies from kitchen to kitchen. The wiener schnitzel here is listed under its French name, escalopes de veau Viennoise, or Viennese-style.

Escalopes de Veau à l'Anglaise

(Breaded veal scaloppine)

4 servings

4 thin slices veal (scaloppine), about 1½ pounds
Salt and freshly ground pepper to taste
2 tablespoons flour
1 large egg, beaten
2 tablespoons water
1½ cups fine fresh bread crumbs
3 tablespoons oil, plus more as necessary
1 tablespoon butter, plus more as necessary
4 tablespoons Demi-glace (page 197), or canned beef gravy (optional)
4 tablespoons Beurre Noisette (page 202) (optional)
Parsley sprigs for garnish

1. Pound the meat with a flat mallet and sprinkle with salt and pepper.

2. Dredge the meat, one slice at a time, first in flour, then in egg beaten with the water, and finally in bread crumbs. As each piece is breaded, transfer to a flat surface and tap lightly with the flat side of a heavy kitchen knife to help crumbs adhere.

3. Heat the oil and butter in a heavy skillet and cook the meat to brown on one side. If the skillet is not large enough to hold the meat in one layer, this will have to be repeated two or more times. When the veal is brown on one side, turn and cook to brown on the other side. Total cooking time for each slice should be from three to five minutes, depending on the thickness of the meat. If necessary, add a little more oil and butter to the skillet until all pieces are cooked.

4. Place one slice of veal on each of four serving dishes. Surround each serving with one tablespoon of hot demi-glace and pour one tablespoon of sizzling beurre noisette over each serving. Garnish with a sprig of parsley.

5. Serve with Skillet Potatoes (page 214).

Escalopes de Veau Milanaise

(Breaded veal scaloppine with Parmesan cheese)

Prepare the recipe for Escalopes de Veau à l'Anglaise (above). Use one-fourth cup of freshly grated Parmesan cheese and one and one-fourth cups of bread crumbs rather than just the bread crumbs. Serve with Spaghetti with Marinara Sauce (page 210).

Escalopes de Veau Holstein

(Breaded veal scaloppine with fried egg)

Prepare the recipe for Escalopes de Veau à l'Anglaise (above). Add one egg cooked sunny side up atop each serving. Garnish around the yolk of each egg with four flat anchovies. Spoon demi-glace and beurre noisette around each serving.

Escalopes de Veau Viennoise

(Breaded veal scaloppine with anchovies and capers)

4 servings

1 hard-cooked egg
4 flat anchovies
4 thin, seeded lemon slices
4 Escalopes de Veau à l'Anglaise (above)
4 tablespoons Beurre Noisette (page 202) (optional)

¼ cup chopped onion
4 teaspoons chopped parsley
4 teaspoons drained capers
4 tablespoons Demi-glace (page 197) (optional)

1. Do not prepare the veal until you have the garnishes ready.

2. Chop the egg white finely. Put the yolk through a fine sieve.

3. Roll each anchovy in a circle and place each in the center of a lemon slice.

4. Cook the scaloppine as in the recipe for Escalopes de Veau à l'Anglaise.

5. Arrange the veal slices on each of four serving plates. Spoon the beurre noisette over the veal. In the center of each slice of veal, place an

anchovy-topped lemon slice. Garnish the meat with equal portions of chopped white and sieved yolk, chopped onion, chopped parsley, and capers.

6. If desired, spoon equal amounts of hot demi-glace to the side of each serving.

7. Serve with boiled potatoes.

Escalopes de Veau Zingara

(Breaded veal scaloppine with mushrooms and meats)

4 servings

1 tablespoon butter
1 tablespoon finely chopped shallots
1 cup thin julienne strips of fresh mushrooms
¼ cup Madeira
1 cup Demi-glace (page 197) or canned beef gravy
½ teaspoon arrowroot
½ cup thin julienne strips of cooked tongue

½ cup thin julienne strips of boiled ham
1 small truffle, sliced and cut into julienne strips
4 Escalopes de Veau à l'Anglaise (page 62)
4 tablespoons Beurre Noisette (page 202)
4 teaspoons finely chopped parsley

1. Before cooking the scaloppine, prepare the zingara sauce.

2. Melt one tablespoon of butter in a small skillet and add the shallots. Cook briefly and add the mushrooms. They will wilt and give up their juices. Cook until juice evaporates.

3. Add the Madeira and cook down over high heat, about two minutes.

4. Add the demi-glace and arrowroot and simmer about five minutes.

5. Add the tongue, ham, and truffle and stir.

6. Cook the veal according to the recipe for Escalopes de Veau à l'Anglaise.

7. Spoon the sauce over the bottom of each of four serving plates. Top with breaded veal scaloppine. Pour the noisette butter over the meat, sprinkle with chopped parsley and serve.

8. Serve with boiled potatoes.

Escalopes de Veau aux Champignons

*(Breaded veal scaloppine with
mushroom sauce)*

4 servings

1 tablespoon butter
1 tablespoon finely chopped
  shallots
1½ cups thinly sliced
  mushrooms
1 tablespoon flour
¾ cup Veal Broth (page 197) or
  chicken broth
½ cup heavy cream

Salt and freshly ground pepper
  to taste
Pinch of cayenne pepper
⅛ teaspoon freshly grated nutmeg
4 Escalopes de Veau à l'Anglaise
  (page 62)
4 tablespoons Beurre Noisette
  (page 202)

1. Before cooking the scaloppine, prepare the mushroom sauce.

2. Melt the butter in a saucepan and add the shallots, stirring briefly. Add the mushrooms. The mushrooms will give up their liquid. Cook until most of the liquid evaporates.

3. Sprinkle with flour, stirring with a wire whisk. When blended, add the veal broth, stirring rapidly with the whisk. When blended and smooth, add the cream, salt, and pepper. Stir and cook about five minutes. Add the cayenne and nutmeg.

4. Cook the scaloppine as in the recipe for Escalopes de Veau à l'Anglaise.

5. Spoon equal amounts of the mushrooms over the bottom of four hot plates. Top each with a breaded veal scaloppina. Spoon the beurre noisette over the scaloppine.

6. Serve with boiled potatoes.

Veal Cutlet Parmigiana

4 servings

4 Escalopes de Veau à l'Anglaise
  (page 62)
2 cups marinara sauce (page 210)

4 ¼-inch-thick slices mozzarella
½ cup freshly grated Parmesan
  cheese

1. Cook the veal as for escalopes de veau à l'anglaise.

2. Arrange the veal in one large or individual baking dishes. Cover each slice with and equal amount of marinara sauce. Top with one slice of mozzarella. Sprinkle with Parmesan.

3. Bake at 450 degrees until the cheese melts. Run under the broiler to glaze.

There are many names for this dish, depending on the country in which it is made. These pieces of rolled veal are sometimes called oiseaux sans têtes, which means birds without heads. In Italian, they are called ucceletti.

Oiseaux sans Têtes

(Stuffed veal birds)

4 to 8 servings

1 pound loose fresh spinach or 1
  10-ounce package
5 tablespoons butter
3 tablespoons finely chopped
  onion
1 teaspoon finely minced garlic
1 cup finely chopped
  mushrooms
Salt and freshly ground pepper
  to taste
½ pound ground pork
1 egg
¾ cup fresh bread crumbs

⅛ teaspoon grated nutmeg
1 tablespoon freshly grated Parmesan cheese
8 slices veal (scaloppine), about
  1½ pounds
Flour for dredging
½ pound mushrooms, thinly
  sliced
1 tablespoon dried tarragon
½ cup dry white wine
1 cup fresh or canned chopped
  tomatoes

1. Preheat the oven to 375 degrees.

2. Rinse the spinach and put it in a saucepan. Cover and let it cook in the water that clings to the leaves. Drain and cool. Press between the hands to remove most of the excess moisture. Coarsely chop spinach.

3. Heat one tablespoon of butter in a saucepan and add two tablespoons chopped onion, half the garlic, and all the chopped mushrooms. Sprinkle with salt and pepper and cook about five minutes. Add the spinach and stir to blend.

4. Put the pork in a mixing bowl and add the egg, bread crumbs, nutmeg, Parmesan, spinach mixture, salt, and pepper.

5. Pound the veal slices with a flat mallet.

6. Spoon equal parts of the spinach filling in the center of each slice. Roll jellyroll fashion. Tie each roll in several places with string. Sprinkle with salt and pepper and dredge lightly in flour.

7. Heat the remaining butter in one large or two medium skillets and add the veal rolls. Brown on one side, about five minutes, then turn and brown lightly on the other. Scatter the sliced mushrooms, tarragon, the remaining tablespoon of chopped onion, and the remaining garlic over all. Bake fifteen minutes and add the wine and tomatoes.

8. Put the skillet on top of the stove and bring the sauce to the boil. Turn the rolls in the liquid and sprinkle with salt and pepper. Cover with a round of wax paper and bake thirty minutes. Cut off and discard the strings.

9. Serve with the skillet sauce and Buttered Fine Noodles. (page 209).

•Steaks•

Although this chapter is labeled "steaks," it actually embraces several preparations of veal that would not fit into the popular concept of a steak: that is to say, a rather large, flat, and somewhat thick cut of meat. A steak of that description can be tailored by cutting it down to size into medallions, which might be said to mean small steaks, and grenadins, which are even smaller. All these terms are, of necessity, somewhat vague, and the thickness and weight of the steak, medallion, or grenadin will vary from recipe to recipe.

Recipes in this category are international, in both scope and flavor. There is a paprika schnitzel from Germany; there are veal steaks with green peppercorns from France; there are grenadins of veal in almond sauce from Mexico; there is a lombatina of veal from Italy; and there is even a dish created by a Chinese chef, veal slices Hunan-style.

Like many other parts of veal, steaks depend to a great extent on quick cooking. When overcooked, these cuts tend to be dry and uninteresting. Steaks, by the way, are cut from the loin or the leg.

Special mention should be made of one dish in this group. It is the paillarde of veal, whose very essence depends on the speed with which it is grilled. And, if anyone cares, it is wildly low in calories. Each serving demands about one teaspoon of butter. The only other seasonings are salt, pepper, and lemon juice. It is a soaringly good dish.

This recipe is from the Café Argenteuil in New York.

Médaillons de Veau Argenteuil

(Veal medallions with mushrooms and foie gras)

4 servings

4 slices veal cut from the loin, about 1½ pounds
½ pound fresh mushrooms
Juice of half a lemon
5 tablespoons butter
½ cup heavy cream
Salt and pepper
1 tablespoon finely chopped shallots

¼ cup Madeira
½ cup Demi-glace (page 197) or canned beef gravy
2 tablespoons chopped truffles
⅓ cup foie gras cut into ½-inch cubes
4 thin slices Gruyère or Swiss cheese

1. Place the veal slices between sheets of plastic wrap and pound lightly with a flat mallet.

2. Coarsely chop the mushrooms and add them to the container of a food processor. Sprinkle with lemon juice. Blend the mushrooms to a purée.

3. In a small skillet, heat two tablespoons of butter and add the puréed mushrooms. Add the cream and stir. Add salt and pepper to taste. Bring to the boil and cook, stirring occasionally, until the mixture is thickened and spreadable.

4. Heat three tablespoons of butter in a large skillet and add the veal slices. Cook four or five minutes on one side. Turn the slices and cook four or five minutes on the other. Do not overcook.

5. Transfer the slices to a warm platter and add the shallots to the skillet. Add the wine and cook until reduced by half. Add the demi-glace. Bring to the boil. Strain the sauce through a very fine sieve. Add the truffles and foie gras.

6. Heat the mushroom mixture and spoon equal portions of it on top of each veal slice. Cover each portion with a slice of cheese and run briefly under the broiler until cheese melts.

7. Serve with equal amounts of the hot sauce spooned on top of and around each serving.

8. Serve with Braised Celery (page 217).

This recipe is from Buca Lapi restaurant in Florence, Italy.

Lombatina di Vitello di Latte

(Veal steak with mushrooms and white wine)

4 servings

1½ pounds veal steak taken
   from the loin
Salt and freshly ground pepper
   to taste
2 tablespoons butter
1 tablespoon olive oil
2 teaspoons finely minced garlic
1 tablespoon chopped fresh
   mint leaves or 1 teaspoon
   dried

½ pound mushrooms, cut into
   ½-inch thick rounds
¼ cup water
½ cup dry white wine
2 tablespoons heavy cream

1. Cut the meat into four pieces of approximately equal size. Sprinkle with salt and pepper.

2. Heat the butter in a heavy skillet and cook the meat until nicely browned on both sides. Continue cooking, about five minutes to a side.

3. Meanwhile, heat the oil in a saucepan and add the garlic and mint. Cook briefly and add the mushrooms and salt and pepper to taste. Cook, stirring, about five minutes and add one-quarter cup water. Cover and cook ten minutes.

4. When the veal is almost done, add half a cup of dry white wine. Continue cooking until wine evaporates.

5. Add the mushroom mixture to the meat. Cook the sauce down briefly and add the cream. Continue cooking until the sauce is slightly thickened. Serve hot.

6. Serve with spinach cooked in butter and olive oil and seasoned with lemon.

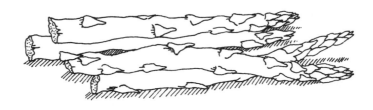

This recipe is from the Four Seasons in New York.

Sauté of Veal with Mushrooms and Crabmeat

6 servings

6 boneless veal steaks, taken
    from the loin or saddle
Salt and freshly ground pepper
    to taste
6 large mushrooms, about
    ¼ pound

5 tablespoons salted butter
2 tablespoons water
⅓ pound fresh lump crabmeat

1. Place the veal steaks on a flat surface and pound lightly with a flat mallet. When ready, they should be about three-quarters of an inch thick. Sprinkle with salt and pepper.

2. Remove the stems of the mushrooms. Slice the mushrooms as thinly as possible.

3. Heat two tablespoons of the butter in a heavy skillet and add the steaks, cooking over high heat. Cook about two minutes and turn.

4. Reduce the heat and cook about four minutes. Turn the steaks once more and cook about one minute longer.

5. Transfer the steaks to a warm platter. Add two tablespoons water to the skillet and stir. Pour this sauce over the veal.

6. Heat one tablespoon of butter in a heavy skillet and add the mushroom slices. Cook, stirring and tossing, about two minutes. Pour the mushrooms over the veal.

7. Add two tablespoons of butter to the skillet and add the crabmeat. Cook, tossing and stirring gently, just until crabmeat is heated through. Pour the crabmeat over the veal. Serve hot.

8. Accompany with Carrots Vichy (page 218).

It was noted earlier that this is one of the great cuisine minceur dishes of all times. It consists of a veal steak quickly seared and seasoned with a minimum of butter, salt, and pepper and served with a lemon wedge. This recipe may also be made with a ½-pound veal chop pounded to a quarter-inch thickness. Gastronomic encyclopedias speculate that the name originated many decades ago in Paris. One of the town's leading restaurateurs was a Monsieur Paillard.

Paillarde de Veau

(Flattened grilled veal steak)

1 serving

½ pound thinly sliced veal steak
Salt and freshly ground pepper
   to taste

Oil for brushing meat
1 teaspoon butter
Lemon wedge

1. The crucial elements in cooking this dish are speed and high heat. Ideally, the paillarde should be cooked on a hot grill, but a very hot skillet will do.

2. Place the veal between sheets of plastic wrap and pound it with a flat mallet until it is about one-fourth inch thick.

3. Sprinkle the meat with salt and pepper and brush with about one tablespoon of oil on all sides.

4. Meanwhile, if a grill is to be used, fire it well. It must have an intense heat. Or heat a heavy iron skillet large enough to hold the meat so that it will cook quickly and evenly. The skillet must be intensely hot.

5. If a grill is used, place the steak diagonally on the grill and cook it about ten seconds on one side. Give it a half turn on the grill (on the same side) in order to give it a diamond pattern. Cook ten seconds and turn the meat over. Cook ten seconds and give it a half turn to make a pattern on the other side. Cook ten seconds.

6. If a skillet is used, add the meat when it is very hot and cook about thirty seconds. Turn the meat over and cook fifteen seconds on the other side.

7. Place the meat on a hot plate and rub the butter over it. Serve with lemon wedge.

8. Grilled Tomatoes with Oregano (page 217) and Potatoes in Cream Sauce (page 214) go well with this.

This recipe is from "21" in New York.

Médaillons de Veau Charleroi

(Veal steaks glazed with a mushroom purée)

4 servings

1½ pounds veal, cut into 4 slices
4 tablespoons butter
¼ cup finely chopped onion
¼ pound mushrooms, coarsely chopped
¼ teaspoon rosemary
½ bay leaf
¼ cup raw long-grain rice
¾ cup water
Salt and freshly ground pepper

1 egg yolk
4 tablespoons freshly grated Parmesan cheese
2 tablespoons flour
¼ cup Madeira
½ cup Demi-glace (page 197) or canned beef gravy
½ cup unsweetened whipped cream

1. Preheat the oven to 400 degrees.

2. Pound the veal with a flat mallet and set aside.

3. Melt one tablespoon of butter in a saucepan, add the onion, and cook briefly, stirring. Add the mushrooms and cook about five minutes, stirring. Add the rosemary and bay leaf. Cover and cook ten minutes.

4. Add the rice, water, salt, and pepper. Cover and place in the oven. Bake twenty-five minutes or until rice is tender.

5. Put the mixture in the container of a food processor or blender and blend. Spoon the mixture into a bowl. Stir in the egg yolk and half the Parmesan.

6. Sprinkle the veal with salt and pepper. Dredge lightly in flour.

7. Melt two tablespoons of the butter in a skillet and brown the meat on both sides, about ten minutes in all. Remove the veal to a shallow baking dish and keep warm.

8. Preheat the broiler.

9. To the skillet, add the Madeira and stir to dissolve the brown particles that cling to the bottom and sides of the pan. Add the demi-glace and stir to blend. Strain into a saucepan.

10. Fold the whipped cream into the rice mixture. Spoon the mixture evenly on top of each piece of veal. Round it off and smooth over. Sprinkle with the remaining cheese.

11. Brown under the broiler until nicely glazed.

12. Heat the sauce and swirl in the remaining tablespoon of butter. Pour the sauce around the veal.

13. Serve with Braised Celery (page 217).

This recipe is from Le Bec Fin restaurant in Philadelphia.

Médaillons de Veau Cubat

(Medallions of veal with puréed mushrooms)

4 servings

16 thin slices veal, about
   1½ pounds
Salt and freshly ground pepper
   to taste
¾ cup Duxelles (see recipe)
¼ pound ham, chopped

2 tablespoons butter
½ cup dry vermouth
½ cup heavy cream
½ cup Veal Broth (page 197) or
   chicken broth

1. Pound the veal pieces with a flat mallet. Sprinkle with salt and pepper.
2. Prepare the duxelles and add the chopped ham. Cook briefly. Keep warm.
3. Melt the butter in a large, heavy skillet and cook the veal over high heat until golden brown on both sides, about two minutes or less to a side. Remove and keep warm.
4. Add the vermouth to the skillet and cook to reduce it by half. Add the cream and broth and cook down about five minutes.
5. Meanwhile, make a "sandwich," spreading half the veal slices with equal portions of the duxelles mixture. Top with the other veal slices. Strain the simmering sauce over the "sandwiches" and serve immediately.
6. Serve with Braised Celery (page 217) or Braised Fennel (page 216).

Duxelles

About ¾ cup

½ pound mushrooms, finely
   chopped, about 2 cups
1 tablespoon butter
1 tablespoon finely chopped
   shallots

Salt and freshly ground pepper
   to taste
Juice of half a lemon
1 tablespoon finely chopped
   parsley

1. Prepare the mushrooms the moment before you are ready to cook them or they will darken.
2. Heat the butter and add the shallots. Cook briefly and add the mushrooms, salt, and pepper. Cook until the mushrooms give up their liquid. Add the lemon juice. Continue cooking until the liquid evaporates.
3. Add the parsley and stir.

This recipe is from the Coach House in New York.

Mignonettes of Veal with Glazed Chestnuts

4 servings

12 slices veal cut into 1-inch-
thick slices, about 1½ pounds
total weight
12 small white onions, peeled
½ cup water
¼ teaspoon sugar
Salt to taste
4 tablespoons butter
2 tablespoons flour
Freshly ground pepper to taste

¼ pound mushrooms, thinly
sliced, about 2 cups
2 cooked, thinly sliced artichoke
bottoms
½ cup dry red wine
½ cup Demi-glace (page 197)
(see note)
8 whole cooked chestnuts (see
note)
Chopped parsley for garnish

1. Have the meat cut and ready to cook.

2. Combine the onions, water, sugar, and salt, add one tablespoon of the butter and bring to the boil. Cover and cook ten minutes, or until onions are tender.

3. Uncover and cook over high heat until liquid evaporates and onions are lightly browned and glazed.

4. Dredge the meat on all sides in flour seasoned with salt and pepper.

5. Heat three tablespoons of butter in a heavy skillet large enough to hold the meat in one layer. Add the meat and cook until golden, three or four minutes to a side.

6. Remove and arrange the pieces of veal on a warm platter. Add the mushrooms and artichokes to the skillet and cook briefly. Remove and set aside.

7. Pour off the fat from the skillet. Add the wine and cook, stirring, until almost evaporated. Add the demi-glace and stir to blend.

8. Add the onions, mushrooms, artichokes, and chestnuts to the sauce and bring to the boil. Transfer one chestnut to each mignonette. Pour the remainder of the sauce over the veal and sprinkle with chopped parsley.

NOTE: If demi-glace is not used, substitute half a cup of veal or chicken broth and bring to the boil. Blend half a teaspoon arrowroot with one tablespoon of dry white wine and stir it into the sauce.

Use freshly cooked shelled chestnuts, prepared according to any standard recipe, or use canned chestnuts.

This recipe is from Kemoll's restaurant in St. Louis.

Veal Capricioso

(Breaded veal with herbs and anchovies)

4 servings

1½ pounds veal steaks, about ¾ inch thick
4 tablespoons olive oil
½ teaspoon crushed rosemary
½ teaspoon crushed sage
Salt and freshly ground pepper to taste
1 cup fine fresh bread crumbs
5 tablespoons butter at room temperature

4 chopped anchovies or 1 tablespoon prepared anchovy paste
4 slices French or Italian bread, cut on the bias into slices about ¾ inch thick
2 tablespoons dry sherry

1. Cut the meat into four pieces of more or less equal size.

2. Place the veal in a flat dish and add half the oil and the rosemary, sage, salt, and pepper. Turn the pieces to coat. Let stand one hour.

3. Coat the veal pieces on all sides with bread crumbs.

4. Heat two tablespoons of oil and one tablespoon of butter in a large heavy skillet. Cook the meat on both sides to brown. Lower the heat and continue cooking for seven or eight minutes to a side until done. Do not let the coating burn.

5. Blend four tablespoons of butter with the anchovies.

6. Toast the bread on all sides. Butter one side with anchovy butter. Top the anchovy-spread toast with the veal.

7. Add the sherry to the skillet and stir to blend. Strain this over the meat and serve hot.

8. Serve with Creamed Spinach (page 218).

This dish is adapted from the recipe of André Daguin of l'Hôtel de France in Auch, France.

Filets Mignons de Veau au Maïs Acide

(Veal fillets with pickled corn and marjoram)

4 servings

½ cup fresh or canned whole corn kernels
White vinegar to cover
1¼ pounds veal, cut into 12 slices
Salt and freshly ground pepper to taste
1 clove garlic
2 tablespoons olive oil

⅓ cup dry vermouth
2 tablespoons finely chopped shallots
½ cup Demi-glace (page 197) or canned beef gravy
1 cup heavy cream
1 teaspoon chopped fresh marjoram leaves

1. Put the corn in a small bowl and add vinegar to cover. Let stand overnight.

2. Pound the veal slices lightly with a flat mallet. Sprinkle with salt and pepper. Rub each piece with garlic on all sides.

3. Add the oil to a flat baking dish large enough to hold the veal slices in one layer. Add the slices, turning to coat them with the oil.

4. Combine the vermouth and shallots in a saucepan and cook until the liquid has almost evaporated. Add the demi-glace and cream. Cook down about five minutes.

5. Meanwhile, preheat the broiler to high.

6. Place the veal under the broiler and cook one minute. Turn the pieces and cook one minute longer.

7. Drain the corn well and add it to the sauce. Add the marjoram and serve over the veal.

8. Serve with Baked Rice (page 211).

Veal Steaks with Green Peppercorns

4 servings

4 veal steaks, about 2 pounds
3 tablespoons canned green
    peppercorns, available where
    fine imported foods are sold
Salt to taste
3 tablespoons peanut, vegetable,
    or corn oil

4 tablespoons butter
⅓ cup finely chopped shallots
1 cup dry red wine
1 cup heavy cream

1. Pound the veal steaks lightly with a flat mallet.

2. Drain the peppercorns and rinse under cold running water. Crush about a third of the peppercorns and press them on both sides of each steak. Sprinkle with salt.

3. Heat the oil and one tablespoon of the butter in a large, heavy skillet and add the veal. Cook over medium to high heat about five minutes, or until nicely browned on one side.

4. Turn the steaks and cook eight to ten minutes longer. Remove the meat and keep it warm.

6. Pour off the fat from the skillet and add a tablespoon of butter and the shallots. Cook briefly, stirring, and add the wine. Cook over high heat, stirring, until most of the wine is reduced, five to ten minutes.

7. Add the cream and stir. Boil vigorously about two minutes and add any liquid that has accumulated around the veal steaks. Add the remaining peppercorns, more or less, to taste. Simmer about five minutes and swirl in the remaining two tablespoons of butter.

8. Slice the steak diagonally and spoon the sauce over.

9. Serve with Baked Rice (page 211).

This recipe is from the Firehouse in Sacramento, California.

Firehouse Veal Steak

4 to 6 servings

1½ pounds veal steak, cut into 1-inch cubes
Salt and freshly ground pepper to taste
4 tablespoons butter
3 tablespoons chopped onion

½ pound sliced mushrooms, about 3 cups
2 tablespoons flour
½ cup dry white wine
1 cup sour cream

1. Preheat the oven to 325 degrees.

2. Sprinkle the cubed meat with salt and pepper.

3. Heat the butter in a skillet and cook the cubes of meat, turning often, until golden brown. Transfer the pieces to a dish.

4. Add the onion to the skillet and stir until wilted. Add the mushrooms and cook, stirring, until wilted. Sprinkle with flour and stir. Add the wine. Stir in the sour cream and salt and pepper to taste.

5. Add the meat to the sauce and stir to blend. Cover closely. Bake for one hour.

6. Serve with Buttered Fine Noodles (page 209).

This recipe is from L'Étoile Restaurant in San Francisco.

Médaillons de Veau Normande

(Veal steaks with apples and Calvados)

4 servings

4 veal steaks, about 1¼ pounds total weight
2 firm, ripe apples, about 1 pound
Salt and freshly ground pepper to taste

2 tablespoons flour
3 tablespoons butter
1 tablespoon peanut, vegetable, or corn oil
2 tablespoons Calvados
1 cup heavy cream

1. Place the meat on a flat surface and pound lightly with a flat mallet.

2. Core and peel the apples. Cut them into eighths.

3. Sprinkle the meat with salt and pepper and dredge lightly in flour. Shake to remove excess.

4. Heat two tablespoons of the butter and the oil in a large heavy skillet and add the meat. Brown on both sides, about five minutes to a side.

5. Keep the meat in the skillet but pour off the fat. Add the Calvados and ignite it. Remove the meat and keep warm.

6. Add the cream, salt, and pepper and cook down over high heat, until sauce is thickened and slightly syrupy in texture.

7. Meanwhile, as the meat is cooked and the sauce reduced, heat the remaining butter and add the apples. Sprinkle with salt and cook, tossing and stirring gently, five to ten minutes.

8. Spoon the apples over the meat and strain the sauce over all.

9. Serve with Braised Fennel (page 216).

Although veal is rarely found on Chinese menus, one of the great veal dishes in Manhattan is prepared at the Shun Lee Palace by the chef-owner, T. T. Wang. The dish consists of veal sliced razor-thin, cooked quickly, and seasoned Hunan-style. Which is to say with garlic, ginger, and chili paste.

Veal Slices Hunan-Style

2 to 4 servings

¾ pound veal steak in one piece, about 1½ inches thick
1 egg white
1 tablespoon cornstarch
6 tree ear mushrooms (see note)
3 straw mushrooms (see note), well drained and split in half lengthwise
6 snow peas, ends trimmed
10 slices water chestnuts
½ teaspoon finely chopped garlic
2 teaspoons chopped green onions
½ teaspoon finely chopped fresh ginger

1½ teaspoons chili paste with garlic (see note)
2 tablespoons shao hsing wine (see note) or dry sherry
1½ tablespoons soy sauce
2 teaspoons sugar
⅛ teaspoon monosodium glutamate (optional)
2 teaspoons cornstarch
2 teaspoons water
1 teaspoon red wine vinegar
⅛ teaspoon ground white peppercorns
1 teaspoon sesame oil
4 cups peanut, vegetable, or corn oil

1. Place the veal on a flat surface and cut it into razor-thin slices using a sharp knife. This will be facilitated if the meat is partly frozen before slicing.

2. Put the meat slices in a mixing bowl and add the egg white and cornstarch. Blend well, using the fingers to separate the slices.

3. Soak the tree ears in warm water until they are softened. Drain well and put on a small plate.

4. Add the straw mushrooms, snow peas, water-chestnut slices, garlic, green onions, and ginger. Measure out the chili paste with garlic and set aside.

5. Blend the wine, soy sauce, sugar, monosodium glutamate, cornstarch blended with water, vinegar, white pepper, and sesame oil.

6. Heat the oil in a hot wok and swirl it around to coat the sides. When the oil is very hot but not smoking, add the meat, stirring rapidly using a circular motion, about fifteen seconds. Drain quickly in a colander but leave about one tablespoon of oil in the wok.

7. Add the tree ears, straw mushrooms, snow peas, water chestnuts, garlic, green onions, ginger, and chili paste with garlic, stirring quickly, and cook five seconds.

8. Add the soy sauce mixture and cook, stirring quickly, about ten seconds. Add the meat and toss until hot and coated. Serve immediately.

Note: The tree ears, straw mushrooms, chili paste with garlic, and shao hsing wine are available in Chinese markets.

This recipe is from Haussner's Restaurant in Baltimore.

Paprika Schnitzel

(*Veal steaks with paprika cream sauce*)

4 servings

4 veal steaks, about 1½ pounds	1 tablespoon Hungarian paprika
Salt and freshly ground pepper to taste	1 cup Veal Broth (page 197) or chicken broth
5 tablespoons butter	½ cup heavy cream
½ cup finely chopped onion	1 tablespoon flour

1. Pound the steaks lightly with a flat mallet. Sprinkle with salt and pepper and set aside.

2. Melt three tablespoons of butter in a skillet and add the onion. Cook to wilt and sprinkle with paprika. Cook about two minutes and add the broth. Cook five minutes.

3. Add the cream and simmer about ten minutes.

4. Meanwhile, dredge the veal steaks lightly in flour.

5. Melt two tablespoons of butter in a heavy skillet and brown the steaks on one side over high heat, three to four minutes. Turn and brown on the other. Cook for a total of seven to eight minutes.

6. Strain the sauce over the meat and stir.

7. Serve with Spaetzle (page 210).

This recipe is from Delmonico's restaurant in Mexico City.

Grenadins of Veal
in Almond Sauce

4 servings

2 dried ancho chilies (see note) or 2 teaspoons chili powder
1½ pounds veal steak, cut into 4 pieces
Salt and freshly ground pepper to taste
1 onion, peeled and thinly sliced, about ¼ pound
2 cloves garlic, sliced
¾ cup Veal Broth (page 197) or chicken broth
1 teaspoon toasted cumin seeds, crushed
1 teaspoon cornstarch
2 teaspoons water
⅓ cup whole almonds
2 tablespoons lard or vegetable oil
8 strips sweet green pepper for garnish
8 strips sweet red pepper for garnish

1. If ancho chilies are available, place them in a saucepan and add water to cover. Bring to the boil and simmer two minutes. Let stand, turning the chilies until softened all over.

2. Place the pieces of veal on a flat surface and pound lightly with a mallet. Sprinkle with salt and pepper. Arrange the steaks in one layer and close together in a skillet.

3. Drain the anchos. Remove and discard the stems. Split open and remove and discard the seeds and veins. Put the chilies in a blender or food processor. Add the onion, garlic, and broth. Blend to a purée. Add cumin seeds and salt and pepper to taste.

4. Pour this sauce over the veal steaks. Bring to the boil and simmer ten minutes.

5. Blend the cornstarch and water and stir it into the simmering sauce. Let thicken. Remove the steaks and set aside.

6. Coarsely chop the almonds.

7. Heat the lard in a saucepan and add all but two tablespoons of the chopped almonds. Cook the almonds until lightly browned. Add the chili sauce and cook down briefly over high heat. Pour the sauce over the veal.

8. Serve the veal steaks on individual hot plates with the sauce spooned over. Garnish each serving with a strip of green and red pepper. Sprinkle with the reserved uncooked almonds.

9. Serve with Baked Rice (page 211).

NOTE: Ancho chilies are available where Mexican and Spanish foods are sold.

This recipe is from the Ondine restaurant in Sausalito, California.

Grenadins de Veau Gentilhomme

(Veal steaks with avocado and tomato)

4 to 8 servings

1½ pound veal steak, about ¾ inch thick
Salt and freshly ground pepper to taste
2 tablespoons flour
3½ tablespoons butter
1 cup tomatoes, drained
2 avocados, or 4 if they are very small
3 tablespoons dry sherry

1 tablespoon finely chopped shallots
2 tablespoons Cognac
1 cup Velouté de Veau (page 198)
1½ cups heavy cream
1 egg yolk
½ teaspoon Worcestershire sauce
2 tablespoons whipped cream

1. Cut the veal into eight pieces of equal size. Sprinkle with salt and pepper and dredge all over in flour.

2. Heat two tablespoons of butter in a heavy skillet and add the veal. Brown on both sides over high heat, turning as necessary. This should take five to six minutes in all.

3. Meanwhile, heat the remaining butter in a saucepan and cook the tomatoes about two minutes. Set aside.

4. Peel and quarter the avocados and discard the pits. Arrange one quarter, hollow side up, on each slice of veal. Spoon the sherry around the veal and cover closely. Cook over low heat ten minutes.

5. Carefully transfer the avocado-topped veal slices to a heatproof baking dish.

6. Preheat the broiler.

7. To the skillet in which the veal cooked, add the shallots and cook briefly. Add the Cognac and cook about thirty seconds, stirring. Add the velouté and heavy cream and cook down over high heat, stirring often, about ten minutes. Add salt and pepper to taste.

8. Remove from the heat and add the yolk, stirring rapidly. Add the Worcestershire and the whipped cream and stir rapidly.

9. Spoon a little tomato into each avocado section. Spoon the sauce over. Run under the broiler until nicely glazed and browned.

10. Serve with Braised Endives (page 216).

This recipe is from La Vieille Varsovie in Dallas.

Medallions of Veal with Chanterelles

4 servings

8 slices veal, about 1½ pounds
Salt and freshly ground pepper
   to taste
1 7- or 8-ounce can chanterelles
   (see note), drained
1 tablespoon peanut, vegetable,
   or corn oil

2 tablespoons butter
1 tablespoon finely chopped
   shallots
½ cup port
1 cup heavy cream

1. Pound the veal lightly with a flat mallet. Season to taste with salt and pepper.

2. Drain the mushrooms and set aside.

3. Heat the oil and butter in a skillet and, when it is quite hot, add the veal. Cook quickly one or two minutes to a side, turning once. Transfer to a warm platter.

4. Pour off the fat from the pan. Add the shallots and mushrooms and cook, stirring, about one minute.

5. Add the port and cook down by half.

6. Add the cream and cook down until sauce is thick enough to coat the veal. Add salt and pepper to taste. Pour over veal and serve.

7. Serve with Creamed Spinach (page 218) and Skillet Potatoes (page 214).

NOTE: Imported chanterelles are available in cans in specialty shops that deal in fine imported foods. They are sometimes labeled with the name Pfifferlinge; these come from Germany or Switzerland.

Brochettes of Veal with Rosemary

4 to 6 servings

1¼ pounds lean veal
2 tablespoons peanut, vegetable,
   or corn oil
1 tablespoon red wine vinegar
1 teaspoon chopped rosemary

Salt and freshly ground pepper
   to taste
1 clove garlic, finely minced
Sauce Diable II (page 202)

1. Cut the veal into one-inch cubes and place them in a mixing bowl. Add all the remaining ingredients except the Sauce Diable and stir until well seasoned.

2. Arrange the cubed veal on four to six skewers. If wooden skewers are used, it is best if they are soaked for an hour in cold water.

3. Prepare a charcoal fire in a grill. When the coals and grill are properly hot, brush the grill lightly with oil. Arrange the skewered veal on the grill and cook, turning as necessary, fifteen to twenty minutes.

4. Serve with Sauce Diable and Baked Rice (page 211).

This recipe is from the Blue Horse restaurant in St. Paul, Minnesota.

Veal Florentine Blue Horse

(Spinach-stuffed veal steaks with cheese sauce)

4 servings

4 veal steaks, each about 1 inch thick
Salt and freshly ground pepper to taste
1 pound fresh spinach in bulk or 1 10-ounce package
5 tablespoons butter
½ cup chopped onion
1 teaspoon chopped garlic
4 tablespoons freshly grated Parmesan cheese
6 tablespoons fine fresh bread crumbs
¼ teaspoon grated nutmeg
1 egg plus 2 egg yolks
2 tablespoons flour
1 cup milk
¼ cup heavy cream
¾ cup grated Gruyère or Swiss cheese
¼ cup dry sherry

1. Preheat the oven to 450 degrees.

2. Cut a pocket in each steak to make them suitable for stuffing. Sprinkle the steaks with salt and pepper.

3. Cook the spinach briefly in boiling salted water to cover. Drain. When cool enough to handle, press to extract excess liquid. Chop the spinach coarsely.

4. Heat one tablespoon of the butter and add the onion and garlic. Cook briefly and add the spinach, tossing to heat. Add half the Parmesan cheese and the bread crumbs, nutmeg, egg, one egg yolk, salt, and pepper. Let cool.

5. Heat two tablespoons of butter in a saucepan. Add the flour and stir with a wire whisk. Add the milk, stirring rapidly with the whisk. Add salt and pepper to taste. Cook briefly until thickened and smooth. Add the cream and bring to the boil. Add the Gruyère cheese and stir until

the cheese melts. Add one egg yolk, stirring rapidly. Remove from the heat.

6. Heat the remaining butter in a skillet and add the steaks. Cook to brown on both sides, about one minute to a side. Do not cook the steaks until done.

7. Stuff the steaks. There will be some spinach left over. Arrange the excess on the bottom of a dish large enough to hold the steaks in one layer. Arrange the steaks over the spinach.

8. Blend the sauce with the sherry. Pour it over the steaks. Sprinkle with the remaining two tablespoons of Parmesan cheese and bake twenty minutes.

9. Serve with Buttered Fine Noodles (page 209).

•Breast•

If there is one cut of veal to be found on the tables of rich and poor alike, it is breast of veal. It is found on the menus of small bistros and of luxury restaurants both in France and Italy, as well as in America. This is partly because there is an infinite variety of fine savory fillings with which the breast can be stuffed, and it is a well-known fact that a good stuffing will extend not only the appeal of the veal but also the number of servings of this already relatively inexpensive cut.

The flavors that complement a stuffing for veal breast encompass all manner of meats and herbs and vegetables: mushrooms, spinach, ground pork, bacon, and liver; such cheeses as ricotta and Parmesan; oddments like calf's brains and sweetbreads, and most of the sweet herbs in the garden or on the shelf. Not to mention such universals as shallots and garlic.

Ed Giobbi's Stuffed Veal Breast with Marsala

8 to 12 servings

1 6-pound boned breast of veal
Salt and freshly ground pepper
   to taste
2 cups ricotta cheese
¼ cup freshly grated Parmesan
   cheese
¼ cup finely chopped parsley

2 eggs, lightly beaten
¼ teaspoon grated nutmeg
½ pound ham, thinly sliced or
   cut into ¼-inch dice
1 teaspoon rosemary leaves
2 tablespoons butter or olive oil
1 cup Marsala

1. Preheat the oven to 450 degrees.

2. Place the veal breast skin side down (boned side up) on a flat surface and sprinkle with salt and pepper.

3. In a mixing bowl, combine the ricotta, salt, pepper, Parmesan cheese, parsley, eggs, and nutmeg. The ham may be used in one of two ways. Sliced ham may be arranged over the veal in a thin layer. Cubed ham may be added to the filling. Either method is acceptable.

4. Cover the opened-up breast with the mixture. Roll the breast, jelly-roll fashion. Truss it with needle and string. Take care to sew the opening of the breast as carefully as possible, the stitches close together; otherwise the filling will seep out.

5. Sprinkle the veal with salt and pepper and place it in a shallow roasting pan. Sprinkle with the rosemary and dot with butter. Place in the oven and bake one hour. Do not move the veal during this time, so that the filling will become firm.

6. Add one cup of Marsala to the pan. Cover, reduce heat to 400 degrees, and continue baking one hour longer.

7. Remove the roast from the oven and let stand at least three hours before serving. The dish is best if served the day after it is cooked. Serve cold, cut into half-inch slices.

8. Accompany with Cold Rice Salad (page 213).

This recipe is from the Royal's Hearthside restaurant in Rutland, Vermont.

Stuffed Breast or Brisket of Veal

12 or more servings

1 6-pound boned breast or bris-
    ket of veal
Salt and freshly ground pepper
    to taste
¾ pound veal, cut into cubes
3 egg whites
1 ounce Cognac
½ cup heavy cream
2 ounces foie gras, or first-
    quality liver pâté

2 tablespoons butter
Flour for dredging
½ cup chopped celery
¼ cup chopped carrot
¼ cup chopped onion
1 cup crushed tomatoes
½ cup dry white wine
1 bay leaf
½ teaspoon caraway seeds
¾ cup sour cream

1. Place the breast boned side up on a flat surface and sprinkle with salt and pepper.

2. Put the cubed veal in the container of an electric blender or, preferably, a food processor. If a blender is used, this will have to be done in two or more steps. Add the egg whites, Cognac, cream, and foie gras while processing on high speed. Add salt and pepper to taste.

3. Preheat the oven to 325 degrees.

4. Spread the mousse mixture over the opened-up veal breast. Roll the breast and tie it neatly and compactly with string. Tie a square of foil at each end to keep the filling intact.

5. Heat the butter in a heavy casserole or Dutch oven with a cover. Dust the veal all over with flour and brown it on all sides in the butter.

6. Add the celery, carrot, and onion and cook briefly. Add the tomatoes, wine, bay leaf, and caraway seeds. Cover closely and place the casserole in the oven. Bake two hours, or until roast is well done.

7. Remove the roast. Untie it and discard string and foil.

8. Strain the sauce through a sieve, preferably of the sort known in French kitchens as a chinois. Press the solids with the back of a heavy spoon to extract as much of the juices as possible. Discard the solids.

9. Bring the sauce to the boil. Whisk the sour cream into it, and heat without boiling. Slice the roast and serve with the sauce.

10. Serve with Braised Celery (page 217).

This recipe is from Roger Fessaguet, chef of La Caravelle restaurant in New York.

Tendrons de Veau aux Légumes

(Breast of veal and vegetable stew)

10 or more servings

1 7½-pound breast of veal
½ cup flour
Salt and freshly ground pepper to taste
½ cup peanut, vegetable, or corn oil
1 or 2 ribs celery
4 carrots
3 large leeks

4 tablespoons butter
1 cup chopped onion
2 tablespoons finely chopped shallots
2 cloves garlic, finely minced
2 cups dry white wine
3 cups Veal Broth (page 197) or chicken broth

1. Have the butcher cut and chop the veal breast across the meat and bone into six strips of equal width. Have him cut each of the five longest strips in half. Leave the sixth piece intact.

2. Dredge the pieces in flour seasoned with salt and pepper.

3. Heat the oil in a large, heavy casserole and, when it is very hot and almost smoking, add the veal pieces. Cook, turning as often as necessary to brown well on all sides. This may take twenty minutes.

4. As the meat cooks, prepare the vegetables. Trim and wash the celery, carrots, and leeks. Pat dry. Cut each vegetable into "batons," which is to say pieces that measure about one inch long and one-half an inch wide. There should be about one and one-half cups of celery, two cups of carrots, and three cups of leeks. Set aside.

5. When the veal pieces are browned all over, carefully pour off the fat. Add the butter and, when it melts, add the chopped onion and shallots. Add the garlic and the prepared vegetables.

6. Add the wine and veal broth and cover closely. Simmer two hours. Boil the sauce down over high heat, about fifteen minutes or until thickened.

7. Serve with boiled potatoes.

Cima di Vitello
alla Genovese

(Genoa-style stuffed breast of veal)

12 or more servings

1 5- to 6-pound breast of veal
   with a pocket for stuffing
1 set of calf's brains, about ½
   pound
1 set of veal sweetbreads
Salt to taste
3 tablespoons olive oil or butter
¾ cup finely chopped onion
1 teaspoon finely minced garlic
¼ pound ground veal

Freshly ground pepper to taste
½ pound mortadella, a slice
   about ½ inch thick
4 eggs, well beaten
1 tablespoon chopped fresh
   marjoram or 1 teaspoon dried
¼ cup freshly grated Parmesan
   cheese
1 cup fresh or frozen green peas

1. Wipe the meat and set it aside.

2. Place the brains and sweetbreads in a basin and add cold water to cover. Using the fingers, remove and discard any membranes on the surface of both. Place the brains and sweetbreads in a saucepan and add cold water to cover and salt to taste. Bring to the boil and simmer ten minutes.

3. Drain the brains and sweetbreads and let stand under cold running water until thoroughly chilled. Drain and pat dry. Cut or break the brains and sweetbreads into one-inch cubes or morsels.

4. Preheat the oven to 375 degrees.

5. Heat the oil in a large skillet and add the onion and garlic. Add the ground veal, breaking up the lumps with the side of a metal spoon.

6. Add salt and pepper to taste. Add the pieces of brains and sweetbreads and cook about five minutes. Spoon mixture into a mixing bowl.

7. Cut the mortadella into half-inch cubes (there should be about one cup) and add it to the mixing bowl. Add the eggs, marjoram, salt, pepper, and cheese. Place the mixture in a saucepan and cook, stirring gently, over low heat until the eggs are lightly set.

8. Cook the peas briefly in boiling salted water to cover and drain. Stir them into the egg mixture. Let cool.

9. Open up the veal pocket and stuff with the meat mixture. Sew up the veal. Sprinkle the veal all over with salt and pepper. Lay out a length of heavy-duty aluminum foil and carefully and closely envelop the veal in it. Seal it well. Place the veal in a baking dish and place in the oven. Bake two hours.

10. Remove the foil and serve sliced. Or let cool, refrigerate, and serve cold as a buffet dish.

This recipe is from Fournou's Ovens, the restaurant in the Stanford Court Hotel in San Francisco.

Roast Breast of Veal with Spinach and Aromatic Herbs

12 or more servings

1 7- to 8-pound breast of veal with pocket for stuffing
Salt and freshly ground pepper to taste
¾ pound fresh spinach or 1 10-ounce package
¾ pound bacon
2 tablespoons butter
¾ pound ground veal
1 clove garlic, finely minced
1 tablespoon finely chopped dried rosemary
½ pound cooked ham cut into small cubes
3½ cups finely chopped onions
3½ cups finely chopped mushrooms, about ¾ pound
2 tablespoons finely chopped fresh tarragon or 1 teaspoon dried

1 teaspoon chopped fresh thyme or ½ teaspoon dried
1 cup dry white wine
½ cup Cognac
3 eggs
¾ cup freshly grated Parmesan cheese
3 tablespoons butter
1 cup coarsely chopped onion
1 bay leaf, broken in two
½ cup coarsely chopped celery
1 cup coarsely chopped carrot
3 sprigs fresh thyme or 1 teaspoon dried
2 teaspoons whole rosemary leaves

1. Sprinkle the meat inside and out with salt and pepper and set aside.

2. Drop the cleaned, picked-over spinach into a pan of boiling water, stirring until the water returns to the boil. Drain and let cool.

3. Meanwhile, cut the bacon into small cubes and cook in a skillet until it gives up its fat. Continue cooking until the bacon is slightly crisp. Drain thoroughly.

4. Melt the butter in a large kettle and add the ground veal. Cook, stirring to break up the lumps with the sides of a metal spoon. Add the garlic, chopped rosemary, ham, finely chopped onions, mushrooms, salt and pepper, tarragon, and chopped thyme. Cook about fifteen minutes.

5. Add the wine and cook about five minutes. Add the Cognac and cook until the kettle liquid is almost completely reduced. These ingredients must not be too runny.

6. Squeeze the spinach between both hands to extract excess moisture. Chop it. There should be about one cup. Add this to the kettle.

7. Add the bacon and stir to blend.

8. Beat the eggs and add the Parmesan cheese. Blend well. Add this to the spinach mixture. Add salt and pepper to taste. Bring to the boil, stirring. Remove from the heat and let cool.

9. Preheat the oven to 375 degrees.

10. Stuff the breast of veal with the mixture and arrange the breast, bone side down, in a roasting pan. Sprinkle with salt and pepper and rub or dot with butter.

11. Scatter the onion, bay leaf, celery, carrot, thyme sprigs, and rosemary leaves around the roast. Place in the oven and bake forty-five minutes. Cover loosely with foil and bake one hour and fifteen minutes longer, basting occasionally.

12. Serve sliced with Skillet Potatoes (page 214).

Poitrine de Veau Farcie aux Épinards

(Breast of veal with spinach stuffing)

12 or more servings

1 8- to 9-pound breast of veal with a pocket for stuffing	Salt and freshly ground pepper to taste
½ pound fresh spinach	3 tablespoons butter
1 pound ground pork	4 to 6 ribs celery, cut into ½-inch cubes, about 1½ cups
2 cups chopped onion	
2 cloves garlic, finely minced	2 carrots, cut into ½-inch cubes
½ pound mushrooms, finely chopped	1 large onion, coarsely chopped
	2 cloves garlic, coarsely chopped
2 sprigs fresh thyme, finely chopped, or ½ teaspoon dried	1 whole bay leaf
	2 whole sprigs fresh thyme or 1 teaspoon dried
1 bay leaf, chopped	4 cups canned Italian peeled tomatoes
1½ cups fresh bread crumbs	
3 eggs, lightly beaten	

1. Wipe the meat well with a damp cloth.

2. Rinse the spinach well and cook, covered, in the water that clings to the leaves. Bring to the boil and cook about thirty seconds. Drain well and, when cool enough to handle, squeeze it to extract excess moisture. Chop it and set aside.

3. Put the pork in a deep saucepan and add two cups chopped onion and the finely minced garlic. Cook, stirring, about five minutes and add the mushrooms, chopped thyme, and chopped bay leaf. Cook, stirring

occasionally, about fifteen minutes. Add the chopped spinach and stir to blend well. Remove from the heat. Stir in the bread crumbs and add the beaten eggs, salt, and pepper. Stir and let cool.

4. Meanwhile, preheat the oven to 400 degrees.

5. Stuff the veal with the spinach mixture and sew up the pocket all around to enclose the filling. Sprinkle the meat on all sides with salt and pepper.

6. Heat the butter in a heavy skillet or roasting pan and add the veal, fat side up, bone side down. Bake fifteen minutes and turn the meat skin side up. Bake fifteen minutes longer.

7. Scatter the celery, carrots, coarsely chopped onion, coarsely chopped garlic, whole bay leaf, whole thyme sprigs, and tomatoes around (not on top of) the meat. Cover closely with foil and bake one hour.

8. Reduce the oven heat to 350 degrees. Uncover the meat and bake thirty minutes longer. Let stand about ten minutes before slicing.

9. Serve with Braised Endives (page 216).

Poitrine de Veau Farci

(*Breast of veal with liver stuffing*)

20 servings

4 tablespoons olive oil
2½ cups chopped onion
2 cloves garlic, finely minced
1 cup finely chopped celery
½ pound mushrooms, cut into small cubes, about 2 cups
Salt and freshly ground pepper to taste
1 pound ground pork
½ pound chicken livers, coarsely chopped
1 cup ricotta cheese
½ cup finely chopped parsley
3 large egg yolks

¼ cup freshly grated Parmesan cheese
½ teaspoon grated nutmeg
1 8-pound unboned breast of veal with a pocket for stuffing
3 whole cloves garlic, unpeeled
1¾ cups coarsely chopped onion
1½ cups cubed carrots
1 cup dry white wine
2 cups tomatoes, cubed or crushed
1 bay leaf
4 sprigs fresh thyme or 1 teaspoon dried

1. Preheat the oven to 375 degrees.

2. Heat half the oil in a skillet and add the onion, minced garlic, celery, mushrooms, salt and pepper to taste. Cook, stirring, until onion wilts and much of the moisture evaporates.

3. Place the pork and livers in a bowl and add the vegetable mixture. Add the ricotta, parsley, egg yolks, Parmesan cheese, nutmeg, and salt

and pepper to taste. Stuff the veal breast with the mixture. Using a truss-ing needle, sew up the breast wherever necessary to enclose the filling. Sprinkle the breast on all sides with salt and pepper.

4. Rub a shallow roasting pan with the remaining oil and add the breast, bone side up. Roast uncovered one hour and pour off the fat.

5. Turn the breast bone side down and add the whole garlic, coarsely chopped onion, and carrot. Bake thirty minutes and pour the wine and tomatoes around the veal. Add the bay leaf, thyme, salt, and pepper to the tomatoes. Cover with foil and bake one and one-half hours longer.

6. Pour off the pan liquid and skim off the fat. Serve the veal sliced with the hot pan liquid. This roast is also delicious served cold.

7. Serve with Carrots Vichy (page 218).

Pot au Feu with Stuffed Veal Breast

12 or more servings

1 5¾-pound breast of veal with a pocket for stuffing
1 tablespoon butter
½ pound button mushrooms, sliced
2 cloves garlic, thinly sliced
1½ bay leaves
3 sprigs fresh thyme
¼ pound chicken livers
1 cup loosely packed parsley leaves (the tops of about 20 sprigs)
1 large egg
Salt and freshly ground pepper
¾ pound ground pork
1 cup fresh bread crumbs
4 pounds short ribs of beef with bone in one or two pieces, or use brisket of beef
7 quarts water

10 peppercorns
3 allspice
3 whole cloves
10 whole parsley sprigs
1 large onion, peeled and split in half
2 heads of green cabbage, about 1¼ pounds each
1 whole stalk of celery
1½ pounds fresh turnips, about five
¾ pound carrots, preferably small
4 leeks, trimmed
Tomato Sauce II (page 203)
Coarse salt
Assorted mustards, preferably imported
Cornichons (imported small, sour gherkins)

1. Have the veal breast ready and set aside.

2. Heat the butter in a large saucepan and add the mushrooms. Cook, stirring, until they give up their liquid. Add the garlic, half a bay leaf, and two sprigs of thyme and cook, stirring often, about five minutes. Remove and discard the bay leaf and thyme.

3. Spoon and scrape the mixture into the container of a food processor or grind it with a food grinder. Add the livers, parsley leaves, egg, and salt and pepper to taste and process coarsely or grind it. Add the ground pork and break crumbs and process briefly. If a grinder is used, simply blend all the ingredients together without grinding the pork and crumbs.

4. Stuff the veal breast with this mixture and sew the opening securely.

5. Put the beef in a large kettle and add water to cover. Bring to the boil and simmer about one minute. Drain and run under cold water to chill. Rinse the kettle well and return the beef to it. Add the seven quarts of water and remaining sprig of thyme. Add the stuffed breast of veal, salt, remaining bay leaf, peppercorns, allspice, cloves, and ten whole parsley sprigs. Cover and bring to the boil. Let cook one hour.

6. Meanwhile, place the onion, cut side down, in a heavy skillet and let it cook until it is burnt on the cut surface. Add this to the kettle.

7. Pull off and discard the tough outer leaves of the cabbages. Cut away and discard the cores. When the beef and veal have cooked one hour, add the cabbages.

8. Cut off the tops of the celery ribs about six inches from the base. Reserve the tops for another use. Cut the bottom and the ribs into quarters. Rinse well all over until clean. Tie the ribs with string. Add them to the kettle. After the cabbage and celery have been added, continue cooking thirty minutes.

9. Peel the turnips and scrape the carrots and add them to the kettle. Split the leeks almost but not quite through root end. Wash thoroughly between the leaves. Tie with string and add to the kettle. Cover and cook one hour longer.

10. When ready to serve, slice the beef and veal breast (removing the string). Serve everything hot with hot tomato sauce, coarse salt, various mustards, and cornichons on the side.

•Stews•

Although the flesh of veal has a very definite texture and wholly admirable flavor, the character of that flavor is modest, which is to say nonassertive. That is why it is complemented in a most agreeable way by other seasonings, such as herbs and wine, tomatoes, even cheese. The herb may be just a suggestion, such as tarragon or rosemary. It may, however, be such an assertive thing as garlic, green olives, or sauerkraut. To put it another way, the nonassertive nature of veal may bring out the best flavors in other foods.

The use of veal in stews is international (two exceptions being the cuisines of China and Japan). There is veal paprikash of Hungary, the navarins and blanquettes of France, a curried veal that mimics the cuisine of India. Veal cut into small cubes makes an excellent chili, which is perhaps the most American of all dishes.

The best cuts of veal for stew dishes are the shoulder and the breast.

Meurettes

(Veal stew with Burgundy wine)

8 to 12 servings

4 pounds lean veal, cut into 2-inch cubes for stew
Salt and freshly ground pepper to taste
¼ cup peanut, vegetable, or corn oil
1 cup finely chopped onion
1 teaspoon finely chopped garlic
½ cup water
3 tablespoons flour

2 cups dry red Burgundy wine
1 cup Veal Broth (page 197) or chicken broth
1 teaspoon chopped fresh thyme or ½ teaspoon dried
5 sprigs parsley
1 bay leaf
2 whole cloves
2 tablespoons butter
2 cups thinly sliced mushrooms

1. Preheat the oven to 350 degrees.

2. Sprinkle the pieces of veal with salt and pepper.

3. Heat the oil in a large heavy skillet. Cook a few pieces of meat at a time. If you crowd the meat in the skillet, the meat will give up its juices and not brown properly. The pieces should not be touching as they cook. Cook over high heat.

4. As the pieces of meat are well browned, transfer them to a heated heavy casserole or Dutch oven. Continue cooking the meat until all the cubes are browned, which should take about fifteen minutes.

5. Add the onion and garlic to the skillet. Cook, stirring, about five minutes. Transfer to the casserole.

6. Pour off the fat from the skillet. Add the water and stir to dissolve the browned particles that cling to the bottom and sides of the skillet. Set aside.

7. Sprinkle the veal cubes with flour. Add the wine and veal broth and stir to blend. Add the liquid from the skillet. Add the thyme, parsley, bay leaf, and cloves. Cover and bake in the oven for one hour and fifteen minutes.

8. Heat the butter in a large skillet and add the mushrooms. Cook, stirring and shaking the skillet, about five minutes. Add them to the stew.

9. Serve with boiled parsleyed potatoes.

This recipe is from The Farmhouse in Point Townsend, Washington.

Veal Paprikash with Sauerkraut

8 or more servings

3 pounds stewing veal, cut into 1½-inch cubes
2 tablespoons flour
Salt and freshly ground pepper to taste
4 tablespoons butter
2 cups chopped onion
1 teaspoon finely minced garlic
2 tablespoons paprika
2 tablespoons tomato paste
½ teaspoon caraway seeds
2 cups Veal Broth (page 197) or chicken broth
½ cup dry white wine
2 pounds sauerkraut
8 or more tablespoons sour cream

1. Preheat the oven to 400 degrees.

2. Arrange the veal in one layer in a roasting pan (one measuring 18 x 12 inches is suitable). Sprinkle with flour, salt, and pepper. Toss the veal in the mixture and place in the oven. Bake thirty minutes until nicely browned.

3. Melt the butter in a small casserole and add the onion. Cook until wilted.

4. Add the garlic and paprika and stir to blend. Cook briefly. Add the veal, tomato paste, and caraway seeds.

5. To the roasting pan in which the meat cooked, add the veal broth. Stir with a wooden spoon to dissolve the brown particles that cling to the bottom and sides of the pan. Add this to the casserole. Add the wine.

6. Drain the sauerkraut well and reserve half a cup of sauerkraut juice. Add the sauerkraut and reserved juice to the casserole. Cover and bring to the boil. Simmer two hours.

7. Serve with a dollop of sour cream on top of each portion.

8. Serve with Spaetzle (page 210).

Sauté de Veau Antiboise

(Veal sauté with tomatoes)

12 servings

7 pounds boneless shoulder or breast of veal, cut into 2-inch cubes

Salt and freshly ground pepper to taste

5 tablespoons olive oil

3 cups chopped onion

1½ tablespoons finely chopped garlic

2 cups dry white wine

1 sprig fresh rosemary or 1 teaspoon dried

2 pounds tomatoes, peeled, cored, and cut into 1-inch cubes, about 4 cups

¾ cup stuffed green olives, drained

½ cup water

1. Preheat the oven to 375 degrees.

2. Sprinkle the meat with salt and pepper.

3. In a large, heavy skillet or Dutch oven, heat four tablespoons of the oil and add the meat. Cook, stirring and shaking the skillet occasionally, about twenty minutes.

4. Pour off the fat from the skillet or Dutch oven and add the onion and garlic. Stir to distribute the vegetables. Cook about five minutes and add the wine and rosemary.

5. Heat the remaining tablespoon of oil in another skillet and add the tomatoes and salt and pepper to taste. Cook about five minutes and strain, reserving both the tomatoes and the juice. Add the juice to the veal. Set the tomatoes aside.

6. Place the skillet, uncovered, in the oven and bake forty-five minutes. Cover and continue baking one hour longer.

7. Meanwhile, blanch the olives briefly, unless you prefer a stronger flavor. To blanch them, drop the olives into boiling water to cover. Drain immediately under cold water and set aside.

8. When the meat is done, remove the pieces of meat from the skillet. Strain the cooking liquid and carefully skim off all fat from the surface. Return the meat and the sauce to the skillet and add the water. Spoon the tomatoes over the meat and scatter the olives over all. Bring to the boil and simmer ten minutes uncovered. While cooking, skim off the fat as it rises to the surface.

9. Serve with Buttered Fine Noodles (page 209).

Sauté de Veau aux Légumes

(Veal stew with vegetables)

6 to 8 servings

3 pounds stewing veal, cut into 1-inch cubes

Salt and freshly ground pepper to taste

¼ cup flour

2 tablespoons lard

1½ cups finely chopped onion

2 cloves garlic, finely minced

1 cup dry white wine

1 cup crushed imported tomatoes

1 cup Veal Broth (page 197) or chicken broth

2 sprigs fresh thyme or ½ teaspoon dried

1 bay leaf

1 cup carrots cut into 1½-inch lengths

1 cup turnips cut into 1½-inch lengths

¾ cup celery cut into 1½-inch lengths

1 tablespoon butter

¾ pound mushrooms, quartered, or left whole if they are small

1. Sprinkle the veal with salt and pepper and dredge in flour. Shake off the excess.

2. Heat the lard in a large casserole or Dutch oven and add the veal. Cook, shaking the pot and stirring the pieces around so that they brown evenly. This should take fifteen or twenty minutes.

3. Add the onion and garlic and stir. Add the wine, tomatoes, veal broth, thyme, bay leaf, and salt and pepper to taste. Cover and cook about thirty minutes.

4. Meanwhile, drop the carrots, turnips, and celery into boiling salted water to cover for about one minute. Drain well.

5. Heat the butter in a large skillet and add the mushrooms and vegetables. Cook over high heat, stirring and shaking the skillet, for about three minutes. Add to the meat. Stir to blend. Cover and cook about fifteen minutes longer.

6. Serve with Baked Rice (page 211).

Sauté de Veau aux Aromates

(Veal sauté with herbs)

4 to 6 servings

2 pounds of veal, cut into 1½-inch cubes
Salt and freshly ground pepper to taste
2 tablespoons butter
2 tablespoons vegetable or peanut oil
1½ cups thinly sliced mushrooms
1 cup finely chopped onion
¾ cup finely chopped celery
1 teaspoon finely minced garlic
½ cup dry white wine

¼ cup flour
1½ cups Veal Broth (page 197) or chicken broth
1 cup crushed imported tomatoes
1 sprig fresh rosemary or ½ teaspoon dried
2 sprigs parsley
1 bay leaf
12 small white onions or 2 medium onions cut into quarters
2 tablespoons finely chopped parsley

1. Sprinkle the meat with salt and pepper.

2. Heat the butter and oil in a skillet and cook the meat, a few pieces at a time, until browned on all sides. As meat is browned, set it aside.

3. Add the mushrooms, onion, celery, and garlic to the skillet and cook, stirring, until onion is wilted. Add the wine, stirring, and cook to evaporate. Return the meat to the skillet and sprinkle evenly with flour. Gradually add the broth, stirring to blend.

4. Add the tomatoes, rosemary, parsley sprigs, and bay leaf and cover. Cook over low heat about one hour. Add the onions, cover, and continue cooking about forty-five minutes longer or until meat and onions are tender. Serve sprinkled with chopped parsley.

5. Serve with Puréed Potatoes (page 213).

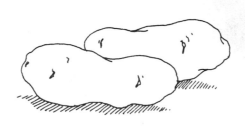

Curried Veal

8 to 12 servings

2 tablespoons butter
4½ pounds lean veal, cut into
    1½-inch cubes
2 cups finely chopped onion
2 tablespoons finely minced gar-
    lic
1 cup finely chopped celery
3 tablespoons curry powder
Salt and freshly ground pepper

2 cups apples cut into half-inch
    cubes
¾ cup banana cut into half-inch
    cubes
2 cups diced peeled tomatoes
2 bay leaves
1 cup Veal Broth (page 197) or
    chicken broth
1 cup heavy cream

1. Heat the butter in a kettle and add the meat, onion, garlic, and celery. Cook, stirring often, without browning, about ten minutes. Add
curry powder and stir to coat the meat.

2. Add the salt, pepper, apples, banana, tomatoes, and bay leaves and
cook about five minutes. Add the broth and cover. Cook one and one-
half hours.

3. Remove the cubes of meat and set aside. Put the sauce through a
food mill and return it to the kettle. Cook down, uncovered, about five
minutes and add the cream. Return the meat to the sauce and cook, uncovered, over moderately high heat about ten minutes, until sauce is
slightly thickened.

4. Serve with Kashmiri Rice (page 212).

This is a recipe from Louis Szathmary of the Bakery restaurant in Chicago.

Tarragon Veal

8 or more servings

4 tablespoons butter
2 cups chopped onions
1 clove garlic
3 teaspoons salt
3 pounds stewing veal, cut into
    1½-inch cubes
1 bay leaf
1 tablespoon finely chopped tar-
    ragon
1 tablespoon sugar

1 cup dry white wine
⅓ cup white vinegar
3 tablespoons chopped flat-leaf
    Italian parsley
½ pound mushrooms, quar-
    tered
4 tablespoons flour
1½ cups milk
1 cup sour cream
Chopped parsley

1. Heat the butter in a casserole and add the onions. Cook, stirring occasionally, until onions are transparent.

2. Combine the garlic and three teaspoons of salt on a flat surface and
chop to a fine purée. Add this to the casserole.

3. Add the veal and stir. Add the bay leaf, tarragon, sugar, white wine, and vinegar and two tablespoons of the parsley.

4. Cover closely and cook over medium heat one hour, or until veal is tender. Uncover and add the mushrooms. Cook briefly three to five minutes.

5. Blend the flour and milk. Add this to the boiling sauce and cook until thickened. Cook about four minutes and add salt to taste. Add the sour cream, stirring constantly. Cook until piping hot without boiling. Serve sprinkled with chopped parsley.

6. Serve with Spaetzle (page 210).

Veal chili with olives and peppers is one of the most curiously appealing dishes that was ever created in our kitchen. It came about simply because one day we found four ingredients on the counter and decided to combine them. There was a quantity of stewing veal, a bottle of chili powder, a bottle of olives, and several sweet peppers. One thing followed another and the end result was eminently edible.

Veal Chili with Olives and Peppers

4 to 6 servings

3 ears corn, cooked
2½ pounds stewing veal, cut into 1½-inch cubes
Salt and freshly ground pepper
¼ cup flour
3 tablespoons lard
1 tablespoon finely chopped garlic
2 tablespoons chili powder
1 tablespoon cumin
2 teaspoons crumbled oregano
3 cups Veal Broth (page 197) or chicken broth
3 green or red sweet peppers
1 tablespoon butter
12 pimento-stuffed olives, each cut in half

1. Cut the corn off the cob. There should be about one and one-half cups. Set aside.

2. Sprinkle the meat with salt and pepper to taste and dredge in flour. Shake off excess.

3. Melt the lard in a skillet large enough to hold the meat in one layer. When it is hot and almost smoking, add the veal pieces and cook until browned all over, about ten minutes. Add the garlic, chili powder, cumin, and oregano. Stir and add the broth, stirring to dissolve the brown particles on the bottom and sides of the pan. Cover and cook about one and one-quarter hours, or until the meat is tender.

4. Meanwhile, split the peppers in half lengthwise and core them. Cut each half into strips about half an inch wide.

5. Melt the butter in a skillet and add the pepper strips and salt and pepper to taste. Cook until crisp-tender. Cover and cook one minute longer.

6. Add the corn, pepper strips, and olives to the veal, stirring to blend. Serve hot.

7. Accompany with Baked Rice (page 211).

This is the recipe of Raymond Vaudard, one of America's most dedicated and respected chefs and an officer of the Chefs de Cuisine Association of America.

Oriental Veal Stew

8 or more servings

¼ cup peanut, vegetable, or corn oil

2 cups chopped onion

2 sweet red and/or green peppers, cut into cubes, about 2 cups

3 pounds stewing veal, cut into 1½-inch cubes

Salt and freshly ground pepper to taste

1 teaspoon loosely packed saffron

2 cups peeled, cored, cubed fresh or canned tomatoes

1 clove peeled garlic, chopped

3 sprigs parsley

1 bay leaf

2 sprigs fresh thyme or 1 teaspoon dried

½ cup dry white wine

1 cup Veal Broth (page 197) or chicken broth

2 tablespoons tomato paste

1. Preheat the oven to 325 degrees.

2. Heat the oil in a casserole and add the onion. Cook until soft and add the sweet peppers and veal. Sprinkle with salt, pepper, and saffron. Stir to blend.

3. Add the tomatoes and garlic. Tie the parsley, bay leaf, and thyme sprigs into a bundle and add it. Add the wine, veal broth, and tomato paste. Stir to blend.

4. Bring to the boil on top of the stove and cover closely. Place in the oven and bake two hours, or until meat is quite tender.

5. Remove the casserole. Pour off the cooking liquid into a saucepan. Set the meat aside.

6. Skim off the fat from the cooking liquid. Cook down the sauce by half over high heat. Pour this over the meat. Reheat and serve with rice.

Two of the most celebrated dishes in French cooking go by the names navarin and blanquette. In almost every case, one duplicates the other. There is this exception: In the navarin, the meat is browned before the stew is made. In a blanquette, the meat is cooked for a brief period, but browning must be carefully avoided.

Navarin de Veau

(*A ragout of veal*)

6 to 8 servings

2¼ pounds lean shoulder of veal, cut into 2-inch cubes and including a few rib bones
Salt and freshly ground pepper to taste
2 carrots
2 ribs celery
1 or 2 white turnips
2 potatoes
2 tablespoons peanut, vegetable, or corn oil

2 cups water
½ cup chopped onion
1 clove garlic, finely minced
½ cup dry white wine
2 tablespoons tomato paste
1 bay leaf
2 sprigs fresh thyme or ½ teaspoon dried
⅓ cup frozen peas (reserve the remaining peas for another use)

1. Sprinkle the meat with salt and pepper and set aside.

2. Trim the carrots, celery, turnips, and potatoes, peeling as necessary. Quarter the carrots and cut them into 1½-inch lengths. Cut the celery into pieces of the same size. Cut the turnips into ½-inch slices. Cut the slices into pieces the same size as the carrots.

3. Cut the potatoes into ½-inch slices. Cut the slices into "sticks" the size of French-fried potatoes. Drop into cold water.

4. Heat the oil in a skillet large enough to hold the meat in one layer. Add the cubes of meat and cook to brown well on all sides, turning as necessary as the pieces give up fat. The browning will take from ten to fifteen minutes.

5. Transfer the pieces of meat to a heavy casserole and heat briefly, stirring.

6. Pour off the fat from the skillet in which the meat was browned. Add one cup of water and stir to dissolve the brown particles that may cling to the bottom and sides of the kettle. Set aside.

7. Add the onion and garlic to the meat and stir. Add the wine and cook briefly. Add the skillet liquid. Add the remaining cup of water, tomato paste, bay leaf, and thyme. Bring to the boil and cook one hour.

8. Meanwhile, cover the carrots, celery, and turnips with cold water and bring to the boil. Drain and set aside.

9. Drain the potatoes. Add them to a saucepan, cover with cold water, and bring to the boil. Drain.

10. When the stew has cooked one hour, add the carrots, celery, and turnips. Cook twenty minutes. Add the potatoes and cook five minutes longer. Add the peas and continue to cook five minutes, or until the potatoes are tender.

Blanquette de Veau

(Veal in a wine and cream sauce)

8 or more servings

4 pounds boneless shoulder of veal
Salt and freshly ground pepper to taste
4 tablespoons butter
1 cup finely chopped onions
1 clove garlic, finely minced
⅓ cup flour
¼ pound mushrooms, rinsed, drained, and quartered
4 large carrots, trimmed, scraped, and cut into ½-inch lengths

1 cup dry white wine
1¾ cups Veal Broth (page 197) or chicken broth
2 sprigs fresh thyme or ½ teaspoon dried
1 bay leaf
12 to 24 peeled small white onions
1 cup freshly shelled peas
1 cup heavy cream
2 egg yolks
¼ teaspoon nutmeg
Juice of half a lemon

1. Preheat the oven to 350 degrees.

2. Cut the veal into one-and-one-half-inch cubes and sprinkle with salt and pepper.

3. In a deep, heavy kettle or Dutch oven, heat two tablespoons of butter and add the veal. Cook, stirring frequently, about five minutes. Sprinkle with the onion and garlic and continue cooking about five minutes. Sprinkle with flour and cook, stirring to distribute the flour evenly, about five minutes.

4. Add the mushrooms and carrots. Add the wine and broth, stirring constantly. Add the thyme, bay leaf, and salt and pepper to taste. Cook ten minutes on top of the stove and cover. Put the dish in the oven and bake about one and one-half hours, stirring occasionally.

5. In a small saucepan, heat the remaining butter and add the white onions and fresh peas. Cover and cook over low heat about fifteen minutes. Add to the veal.

6. Blend the cream with the egg yolks, nutmeg, and lemon juice and stir this into the veal. Cook on top of the stove, stirring, just until the sauce starts to boil.

7. Serve with Buttered Fine Noodles (page 209).

This blanquette de veau has a curious twist. It is a recipe given to us by a friend, Aline Landais, a French decorator now living in Manhattan. When she first outlined this to us, it sounded bizarre, adding cauliflower to such a subtle dish. But it is a truly elegant combination.

Blanquette de Veau Aline Landais

(Veal stew with cauliflower)

8 to 12 servings

5 pounds boneless shoulder of veal
1 medium head of cauliflower
½ pound small white onions, about 16 to 24, peeled (the smaller the onions the better)
1 cup celery cut into small sticks measuring about ½ inch thick and 1½ inches long
½ pound mushrooms, left whole if small or cut into halves or quarters if large
Juice of ½ lemon
7 cups Veal Broth (page 197) or chicken broth

1 medium onion, stuck with 4 cloves
2 whole cloves garlic, unpeeled
1 bay leaf
Salt
½ teaspoon grated nutmeg
1 teaspoon peppercorns
½ teaspoon thyme
1 cup thin carrot rounds
1 cup heavy cream
½ cup sour cream
4 egg yolks
1 tablespoon lemon juice
1 tablespoon lime juice
⅛ teaspoon cayenne pepper

1. Preheat the oven to 350 degrees.

2. Cut the meat into two-inch cubes.

3. Place the meat in a kettle and add cold water to cover. Bring to the boil. When the water boils vigorously, drain the meat and run under cold running water until thoroughly chilled.

4. Cut away and discard the core from the cauliflower. Break the cauliflower into flowerettes, each piece about one and one-quarter inches in diameter. Set aside.

5. Prepare the small onions and celery in separate batches. Prepare the mushrooms and sprinkle with lemon juice to prevent discoloration.

6. Add the cauliflower to a saucepan and add enough veal broth to barely cover. Simmer briefly until tender but still firm to the bite. Drain but reserve the liquid.

7. Cook the onions and then the celery in the cauliflower liquid until barely tender. Drain, reserving the liquid. Bring the mushrooms just to the boil in the same liquid and drain.

8. Return the meat to a kettle and add five cups of veal broth. Add the onion stuck with cloves, whole garlic cloves, bay leaf, salt to taste, and

half the nutmeg. Tie the peppercorns and thyme in a small cheesecloth bag and add it. Bring to the boil on top of the stove. Cover and place in the oven.

9. Bake one hour and add the carrot rounds and celery. Bake thirty minutes longer, or until meat is tender.

10. Pour the cooking liquid from the kettle into a saucepan. There should be about four cups. Cook over high heat and reduce the liquid to three cups. Add one cup of heavy cream. Combine this with the meat and assorted vegetables—the carrot, cauliflower, onions, celery, and mushrooms. Bring to the boil.

11. Blend the sour cream with four beaten egg yolks. Add the remaining nutmeg, lemon and lime juices, and cayenne pepper. Stir this into the liquid around the meat, stirring over gentle heat just until the sauce comes to the boil. Do not boil for more than a few seconds or the sauce will curdle.

12. Serve with Buttered Fine Noodles (page 209).

Fricassée de Veau

(Veal in a cream, wine, and herb sauce)

10 to 12 servings

1 4-pound breast of veal	2 cups Veal Broth (page 197) or
4 pounds stewing veal, cut into	chicken broth
2-inch cubes	1 cup dry white wine
4 tablespoons butter	⅛ teaspoon cayenne pepper
Salt and freshly ground pepper	3 carrots, scraped, quartered,
to taste	and cut into 2-inch lengths
1 onion, finely chopped	36 small white onions, the
¼ teaspoon nutmeg or more to	smaller the better, peeled and
taste	left whole
1 clove garlic, finely minced	¾ pound mushrooms, quar-
6 sprigs fresh thyme or 1 tea-	tered if large or left whole if
spoon dried	small
1 bay leaf	1 cup heavy cream
6 sprigs parsley	6 egg yolks
2 cloves	

1. Cut the breast of veal into two-inch cubes, chopping through the bone. Or have this done by the butcher. The bone is important.

2. Place the cubed breast of veal and the stewing veal in a large mixing bowl and place under the cold-water tap. Let the water run in a trickle for about an hour. This will whiten the meat. Drain.

3. Heat the butter in a heavy casserole and add the meat. Cook five minutes and sprinkle with salt and pepper. Add the chopped onion, half

the nutmeg, and the garlic. Tie the thyme, bay leaf, parsley, and cloves in a cheesecloth bag and add it. Add the veal broth, wine, and cayenne and cover closely. Bring to the boil and cook forty-five minutes.

4. Add the carrots, whole onions, and mushrooms and cook forty-five minutes longer.

5. Drain off about four cups of the cooking liquid and bring it to the boil. Cook over high heat until reduced almost by half.

6. Blend the cream with the egg yolks, salt, pepper, and remaining nutmeg.

7. Add the reduced hot mixture to the egg-and-cream mixture, stirring rapidly. Return this to the veal, stirring, but do not boil or it will curdle. Bring just to the boil. Remove cheesecloth bag.

8. Serve with Baked Rice (page 211).

This recipe is from La Colomba restaurant in Venice.

Veal Stew alla Friuliana

(Veal, vegetable, and wine casserole)

8 to 10 servings

4 pounds lean veal, cut into 2-inch cubes for stew
Salt and freshly ground pepper to taste
¼ cup peanut, vegetable, or corn oil
1 tablespoon olive oil
1 tablespoon butter
1½ cups coarsely chopped carrots

1½ cups coarsely chopped celery
¾ cup coarsely chopped onion
1 clove garlic, finely minced
½ teaspoon dried thyme
½ cup water
½ cup dry white wine
2 cups Veal Broth (page 197) or chicken broth

1. Preheat the oven to 350 degrees.

2. Sprinkle the pieces of veal with salt and pepper.

3. Heat the peanut oil in a large, heavy skillet. Cook a few pieces of meat at a time. If you crowd the meat in the skillet, the veal will give up its juices and not brown properly. The pieces should not be touching as they cook. Cook over high heat.

4. As the meat cooks, heat the olive oil and butter in a Dutch oven or heavy casserole. Add the carrots, celery, onion, garlic, and thyme.

5. As each batch of meat is browned, transfer the pieces to the casserole. Continue cooking the meat until all of it is browned. It should take about fifteen minutes in all. Pour off the fat from the skillet. Add the water and stir to dissolve the brown particles that cling to the bottom and sides of the skillet. Add this to the meat-and-vegetable mixture.

6. Add the wine and veal broth. Cook briefly, stirring. Cover and place in the oven. Bake one and one-quarter hours.

7. Remove the cubes of veal. Put the sauce, vegetables and all, through a sieve, or blend in a food processor. Return the sauce to the casserole and add the veal. Heat through.

8. Serve with Polenta (page 215).

Mediterranean Veal Ragout with Olives

12 or more servings

1 breast of veal with bones, about 4½ pounds
1 3-pound boneless shoulder of veal
Salt and freshly ground pepper
1 cup oil
3 cups coarsely chopped onion
½ cup flour
3 cloves garlic, finely chopped
6 whole cloves
4 cups dry white wine

2 cups water
1 1-pound-12-ounce can tomatoes
1 bay leaf
6 sprigs fresh parsley
2 sprigs fresh thyme or 1 teaspoon dried
24 stuffed green olives
24 imported black olives (see note)

1. Preheat the oven to 375 degrees.

2. Cut, or have the butcher cut, the breast of veal and boneless shoulder into two-inch or three-inch cubes. Sprinkle with salt and pepper.

3. Heat the oil in one or two skillets and cook the meat pieces, a few at a time, to brown all over. As the meat is browned, transfer it to a large casserole. Continue browning the meat until all of it is used.

4. Sprinkle the meat with the onion and flour and stir until the ingredients are evenly coated with flour. Add the garlic, cloves, wine, and water.

5. Drain the tomatoes but reserve both juice and tomatoes. Add the juice to the meat and stir. Set the tomatoes aside.

6. Bring the veal to the boil and add the bay leaf and the parsley and thyme tied together in a bundle. Add salt and pepper to taste and bring to the boil.

7. Bake uncovered for one and one-half hours, stirring occasionally. Chop the reserved tomatoes and add them. Add the olives and bake, skimming the surface of excess fat, about thirty minutes. Remove herb bundle.

8. Serve with Buttered Fine Noodles (page 209).

NOTE: It is important that imported black olives be used in this recipe to achieve the authentic flavor. Some of the best imported black olives available in this country are those from Greece and Italy. It is preferable that they be cured in a liquid brine rather than "oil-cured." Imported black olives may be purchased in most fine food specialty shops as well as in Italian and Greek grocery stores.

This dish has one of the most celebrated histories of any in the French repertoire. There was a battle between Napoleon Bonaparte's troops and those of Austria near the village of Marengo in north Italy. The date was June 14, 1800. After the battle was won, Napoleon was famished and asked his chef to scurry up a meal. The result was veal Marengo, but the original dish has long since been altered. The dish on which Napoleon dined contained, among other things, a fried egg and crawfish.

Veal Marengo
(Veal in a tomato and mushroom sauce)

8 to 10 servings

4 pounds lean veal cut into 2-inch cubes for stew
Salt and freshly ground pepper to taste
¼ cup peanut, vegetable, or corn oil
½ cup water
1 cup chopped onion
1 teaspoon finely chopped garlic
1 cup diced carrots
1 bay leaf
½ teaspoon thyme
¼ cup tomato paste

1 cup plus 2 tablespoons dry white wine
2 cups Veal Broth (page 197) or chicken broth
2 sprigs fresh parsley
2 teaspoons arrowroot or cornstarch
½ pound mushrooms, quartered
1 tablespoon butter
2 tablespoons finely chopped parsley for garnish

1. Preheat the oven to 350 degrees.

2. Sprinkle the pieces of veal with salt and pepper.

3. Heat the oil in a large, heavy skillet. Cook a few pieces of meat at a time. If you crowd them in the skillet, the meat will give up its juices and not brown properly. Cook over high heat.

4. As the veal is well browned, transfer it to a heated heavy casserole or Dutch oven. Continue cooking the meat until all of it is browned. It should take about fifteen minutes to brown all the cubes. Pour off the fat from the skillet. Add the water and stir to dissolve the brown particles that cling to the bottom and sides of the skillet. Set aside.

5. To the casserole, add the onion, garlic, carrots, bay leaf, and thyme. Cook briefly, stirring, and add the tomato paste, one cup of wine, and

117

the veal broth. Add the liquid from the skillet. Stir to blend and add the parsley. Cover and place in the oven. Bake one and one-quarter hours.

6. With a two-pronged fork, transfer the pieces of meat to another casserole.

7. Skim off the fat from the surface of the sauce. Put the sauce through a sieve, pressing with the back of a wooden spoon to extract as much liquid from the solids as possible.

8. Pour the sauce back over the meat and bring to the boil. Blend the arrowroot and two tablespoons of wine and stir it in.

9. Cook the mushrooms in butter, stirring and shaking the skillet, about five minutes. Add them to the stew. Serve sprinkled with chopped parsley.

10. Serve with Buttered Fine Noodles (page 209).

Veal Chili
Texas-Style

4 to 6 servings

2 pounds stewing veal
¼ pound suet or 2 tablespoons
  peanut, vegetable, or corn oil
1 tablespoon finely minced garlic
3 or 4 tablespoons chili powder
1 teaspoon crushed dried
  oregano
1 teaspoon powdered cumin
Salt and freshly ground pepper
  to taste
3 tablespoons masa harina (see
  note) or 2 tablespoons flour
4 to 6 cups Veal Broth (page 197)
  or chicken broth
1½ tablespoons vinegar
1 tablespoon chili paste with
  garlic (see note) (optional)

1. Using a sharp knife, cut the meat into one-half-inch or even smaller cubes.

2. Cut the suet into cubes and put in a heavy skillet or casserole. Cook, stirring, to render the suet of fat. Remove and discard the solid, rendered suet.

3. Add the meat and cook, stirring, just until meat loses its pink color. Add the garlic, chili powder, oregano, cumin, salt, and pepper. Add the salt sparingly.

4. Cook, stirring, about two minutes and sprinkle in the masa harina. Stir to distribute evenly. Add four cups of veal broth, the vinegar, and the chili paste.

5. Cook, partly covered, about one and one-half hours. Stir the chili occasionally and add more veal broth if the chili becomes too thick.

6. Serve with rice.

NOTE: Masa harina is corn flour, a form of finely ground corn meal, that is widely available in Spanish and Mexican markets.

Chili paste with garlic is a standard ingredient in Chinese cooking. It gives an agreeable pungency to American chili. The paste is widely available in Chinese grocery stores and specialty shops that deal in imported foods.

•Shanks•

Not the least agreeable quality of veal is the natural gelatin to be found in its bones. It is this gelatin that permits a diminished use of flour and other starches in much of veal cookery.

The gelatinous nature of veal bones is best exhibited in shanks, and the best known shank-of-veal dish is ossobuco, most closely associated with Milan. Ossobuco is one of the most admired dishes in the cooking of Italy. How nice to gourmandize on a dish so meaty and neatly perfumed with herbs and, classically, grated lemon and orange peel.

Ossobuco is, of course, but one of the great veal-shank dishes. Shanks may be prepared country-style in a stew with vegetables, or with a white-truffle sauce, as in a recipe we found in Rome, or as rouelles, as conceived in the kitchen of l'Auberge du Père Bise in Talloires.

The best shanks, which are the bone from the ankle up through the calf, are from the hindquarters.

This is the recipe of l'Auberge du Père Bise in Talloires, France.

Rouelles de Veau à la Savoyarde

(A shank-of-veal and vegetable casserole)

8 servings

8 pieces meaty veal shanks, cut across the bone into 2½-inch lengths

Salt and freshly ground pepper to taste

¾ cup flour

4 tablespoons butter

2 whole cloves garlic, unpeeled

2 cups onion cut into 1-inch cubes

2 tablespoons finely chopped shallots

½ cup dry white wine

3 cups Veal Broth (page 197) or chicken broth

2 cups cubed tomatoes

6 sprigs fresh parsley

2 sprigs fresh thyme

2 bay leaves

2 leeks, green part only (optional)

16 small "new" red potatoes, about 1¼ pounds, peeled

¾ pound carrots, halved and cut into 1½-inch lengths

16 small white onions, about ¾ pound, peeled

1 pound white turnips, peeled and quartered or cut into eighths

3 tablespoons freshly chopped parsley

1. Sprinkle the pieces of veal shank with salt and pepper. Dredge all over in flour. Shake off excess.

2. Heat three tablespoons of the butter in a large deep skillet or casserole and, when it starts to brown, add the veal. Cook, turning often, to brown evenly on all sides. Add the garlic and onion and cook about twenty minutes in all.

3. Add the shallots, wine, broth, and tomatoes. Bring to the boil.

4. Tie the parsley, thyme, and bay leaves and the green part of the leeks into a bundle with string and add. Cover and cook about forty-five minutes. Add the potatoes and carrots. Turn the pieces of veal, cover, and continue cooking about fifteen minutes.

5. Meanwhile, heat one tablespoon butter in a small skillet and add the onions. Sprinkle with salt and pepper. Cook, stirring often, to brown all over, about ten minutes.

6. Simultaneously drop the turnips into boiling salted water and simmer about ten minutes. Drain.

7. When the meat, potatoes, and carrots have cooked about one hour, add the onions and turnips. Continue cooking twenty to thirty minutes or until the meat and vegetables are tender. Remove the herb bundle.

8. Sprinkle with chopped parsley and serve.

Stinco di Vitello
al Tartufi

(Braised veal shank with
white-truffle sauce)

8 to 12 servings

1 3½- to 4-pound veal shank
Salt and freshly ground pepper
  to taste
2 tablespoons butter
½ cup carrot rounds
½ cup coarsely chopped onion
½ cup chopped celery
1 clove garlic, cut into quarters
1 cup plus 2 teaspoons dry
  white wine
1 cup Veal Broth (page 197) or
  chicken broth

½ cup chopped tomatoes
4 sprigs parsley
1 bay leaf
2 sprigs fresh thyme or ½ teaspoon dried
2 tablespoons white-truffle
  purée (optional), available in
  cans where fine imported Italian foods are sold
1 teaspoon cornstarch

1. Sprinkle the veal with salt and pepper.

2. Heat the butter in a casserole large enough to hold the veal and brown the meat all over until golden, about five minutes.

3. Scatter around it the carrot rounds, onion, celery, and garlic and cook about five minutes. Add one cup of the wine and the veal broth, tomatoes, parsley, bay leaf, thyme, and salt and pepper to taste.

4. Cover closely and cook about two hours, or until fork-tender.

5. Transfer the meat to a warm platter and cover with foil to keep warm.

6. Strain the sauce through a sieve, pushing through as much liquid from the solids as possible, using a heavy metal or wooden spoon.

7. Let the sauce simmer slowly, about ten minutes, and add the truffle purée. Simmer briefly. Blend the cornstarch with the remaining wine and stir it in. Simmer about thirty seconds and remove from the heat. Serve the meat carved.

8. Serve with Buttered Fine Noodles (page 209).

Jarret de Veau en Potée

(Veal shank country-style)

4 servings

1 4½-pound veal shank
2 cloves garlic
1 small cabbage, about ¾ pound, quartered
½ pound small carrots, trimmed and scraped
1 onion, peeled, stuck with 2 cloves
3 leeks, trimmed, split, washed well, and tied with string
1 small heart of celery

2 sprigs fresh thyme or ½ teaspoon dried
2 allspice
6 peppercorns
Salt to taste
4 small potatoes, about ½ pound, peeled
1 or 2 turnips, cut in half or quartered, depending on size
Horseradish Sauce (page 202)

1. Have the butcher saw off the bony end of the shank and reserve it.

2. Puncture the meaty portion of the shank with a sharp knife in eight places. Cut each clove of garlic into four slivers and insert these into the gashes.

3. Put the shank in a kettle with cold water to cover. Add the bone, cabbage, carrots, onion, leeks, celery tied in a bundle with the thyme, allspice, peppercorns, and salt. Bring to the boil.

4. Simmer forty-five minutes and add the potatoes and turnips. Continue cooking forty-five minutes longer, or until meat is quite tender.

5. Transfer the shank to a serving platter. Reserve one cup of broth for the horseradish sauce. Untie the leeks. Discard celery bundle and the piece of bone. Surround the shank with vegetables. Slice the meat and serve with vegetables and horseradish sauce.

This recipe is from the Third Floor Restaurant of the Hawaiian Regent Hotel in Honolulu.

Veal Shanks Third Floor

(Veal in a tomato, Calvados, and cream sauce)

8 to 12 servings

2 veal shanks, carefully boned to produce two slabs of meat, about 4 pounds total weight
Salt and freshly ground pepper to taste
2 tablespoons flour
2 tablespoons peanut, vegetable, or corn oil
2 tablespoons butter
1 cup chopped onion
½ pound mushrooms, quartered, or, if small, left whole

2 cloves garlic, finely minced
2 bay leaves
½ teaspoon dried rosemary
½ teaspoon thyme
½ cup dry white wine
2 tablespoons tomato paste
1½ cups Veal Broth (page 197) or chicken broth
2 tablespoons Calvados
½ cup heavy cream

1. Preheat the oven to 350 degrees.

2. Split the slabs of meat in half lengthwise. Sprinkle with salt and pepper and dredge in the flour.

3. Heat the oil and butter in a large heavy skillet and add the shanks in one layer. Brown well on all sides, about ten minutes.

4. Add the onion and mushrooms and cook briefly, stirring, until onion wilts. Add the garlic, bay leaves, rosemary, thyme, and wine. Bring to the boil, stirring.

5. Blend the tomato paste with one-half cup veal broth and add it. Add the remaining veal broth and salt and pepper to taste. Bring to the boil.

6. Cover and place in the oven. Bake one and one-quarter hours, or until meat is quite tender.

7. Remove the pieces of shanks. Place the skillet over high heat and reduce the liquid, skimming off the surface fat as it accumulates. Cook down by half and add the Calvados and cream and salt and pepper to taste. Return meat to sauce and baste well. Serve the meat sliced with the sauce.

8. Serve with Spaetzle (page 210).

Ossobuco Milanese

(The classic veal shank Milan-style)

6 servings

6 to 8 pieces (about 5½ pounds) meaty slices of veal shank cut across the marrowbone, each slice about 2 inches thick
Salt and freshly ground pepper
Flour for dredging
3 tablespoons olive oil or butter
1½ cups finely chopped onion
½ cup chopped celery
1 cup chopped carrots
2 tablespoons plus 1 teaspoon finely minced garlic
1 teaspoon crushed marjoram
1½ cups dry white wine
2 cups peeled, crushed tomatoes
1 teaspoon finely grated lemon rind
2 teaspoons finely grated orange rind
¼ cup finely chopped parsley

1. Sprinkle the veal with salt and pepper to taste and dredge in flour. Shake off excess.

2. Heat the oil or butter in a heavy skillet large enough to hold the veal shanks, bone upright, in one layer. Brown the veal all over, about thirty minutes.

3. Add the onion, celery, and carrots. Cook, stirring, about five minutes. Add two tablespoons garlic and the marjoram. Stir and add the wine. Cook about one minute and add the tomatoes and salt and pepper to taste. Cover and cook about one and one-quarter hours.

4. Blend the lemon and orange rinds and remaining teaspoon minced garlic. Sprinkle over the veal and stir to blend. Cover and cook fifteen minutes longer. Sprinkle with chopped parsley.

5. Serve with Risotto (page 212).

This recipe is from the kitchen of Mario's restaurant in the Bronx. It is that of the Migliucci family.

Ossobuco

6 servings

4 pounds meaty veal shanks, cut across the bone into 2½- or 3-inch lengths
Flour for dredging
½ cup peanut or olive oil or a combination of both
1 cup finely chopped onion
2 tablespoons finely chopped lemon peel
1 cup carrots cut into tiny dice
¾ cup finely chopped celery
1 cup dry white wine
3 cups Veal Broth (page 197) or chicken broth
2 bay leaves
½ cup Demi-glace (page 197) or canned beef gravy
Salt and freshly ground pepper to taste

1. Dredge the meat on all sides in flour and shake off excess.

2. Heat half the oil in a casserole or Dutch oven and brown the veal on all sides, ten to fifteen minutes.

3. Add the onion, lemon peel, carrots, and celery and cook about fifteen minutes.

4. Add the remaining ingredients and cover. Cook about one hour and ten minutes or until the meat is fork-tender.

5. Serve with Polenta (page 215).

•Ground Veal•

To some minds—sadly mistaken, we might add—ground-meat dishes are a last resort, to be made only when watching the budget. What an unfortunate attitude! Some of the most appealing and sophisticated dishes in the world are made with ground meat, and few such dishes can achieve the excellence of those made with ground veal.

Some of the dishes in this chapter are outstanding examples, and many of them, as might be expected, are of Scandinavian origin. There are several utterly delectable veal patties—one from the famed Operakällaren restaurant in Stockholm, another with fresh tomato sauce from the Italian Pavillion in New York, and Swedish meat patties with a dill sauce of unknown origin.

One of the most interesting dishes is a lettuce leaf stuffed with veal and served in broth, the recipe from a restaurant in Genoa. There are a basic meat loaf, a basic pâté, zucchini stuffed with veal and pine nuts, and two all-American dishes—a Kansas City chili and a San Antonio picadillo, the latter a recipe discovered at a cocktail party some years ago in that town.

The best cuts of veal for grinding are the shoulder and the leg.

Basic Meat Loaf

6 to 8 servings

2½ pounds ground veal, or a
  combination of beef, pork,
  and veal
2 cups fine fresh bread crumbs
¼ teaspoon grated nutmeg
Salt and freshly ground pepper
  to taste
1 tablespoon butter
¾ cup finely chopped onion

1 clove garlic, finely minced
5 tablespoons chopped fresh
  herbs such as parsley and
  dill, or a combination of several
½ cup heavy cream or milk
1 large egg, lightly beaten
Creole Sauce (page 206)

1. Preheat the oven to 400 degrees.

2. Put the meat in a mixing bowl and add the bread crumbs, nutmeg, salt, and pepper.

3. Heat the butter and add the onion and garlic. Cook until the onion starts to turn brown. Cool briefly and add to the meat.

4. Add the herbs, cream, and egg and blend well with the hands. Pack the mixture into a loaf pan measuring approximately 9¼ x 5¼ x 2¾ inches.

5. Bake one hour. Let stand one-half hour before slicing.

6. Serve, if desired, with creole sauce and Puréed Potatoes (page 213).

Veal Meat Loaf with Herbs

8 or more servings

3 pounds ground veal
1 tablespoon butter
1 cup finely chopped onion
2 cups fresh bread crumbs
1 egg, lightly beaten
2 tablespoons finely chopped
  dill
1 tablespoon finely chopped
  parsley
1 cup cooked ham cut into ½-
  inch cubes

¼ teaspoon grated nutmeg
Salt and freshly ground pepper
  to taste
1 cup heavy cream
5 hard-cooked eggs, peeled
10 strips bacon
Sour Cream, Dill, and Tomato
  Sauce (page 205), optional

1. Preheat the oven to 375 degrees.

2. Butter a baking dish that has a small rim.

3. Place the meat in a mixing bowl.

4. Heat the butter and add the onion, cooking until wilted. Add the onion to the meat.

5. Add the bread crumbs, egg, dill, parsley, ham, nutmeg, salt, pepper, and cream. Blend well.

6. Shape half the meat into a long oval and place in the center of the baking dish. Make an indentation down the center to embed the eggs. Trim off the ends of the eggs so that they are flat. Arrange the eggs in a row down the center. Cover with the remaining meat, enclosing the eggs. Smooth over the top.

7. Arrange the bacon, slices slightly overlapping, over the loaf. Place in the oven and bake thirty minutes. Cover with foil and continue baking one hour longer.

8. Let rest about twenty minutes before serving. Serve with the natural pan juices or with sour-cream sauce. Use the pan juices for the sour-cream sauce.

9. Serve with Puréed Potatoes (page 213).

Veal and Mushroom Loaf

8 or more servings

3 pounds ground veal
2 tablespoons butter
1 cup finely chopped onion
1 clove garlic, finely minced
1 cup finely diced celery
1 pound mushrooms, sliced thin

1 cup fine fresh bread crumbs
¼ teaspoon grated nutmeg
1 cup finely chopped parsley
2 eggs
Salt and freshly ground pepper

1. Preheat oven to 375 degrees.

2. Place the meat in a mixing bowl and set it aside.

3. Melt the butter in a skillet and add the onion, garlic, and celery. Cook briefly until onion wilts. Add the mushrooms and cook until mushrooms give up their liquid. Continue cooking until this liquid evaporates. Let cool. Add this mixture to the veal.

4. Add the remaining ingredients. Blend well. Put the mixture into a standard loaf pan (9¼ x 5¼ x 2¾ inches). Smooth it over. Place the pan in a baking dish and pour boiling water around the pan, about one and one-half inches deep. Bake from one to one and one-quarter hours. Serve hot or cold.

5. Serve with Carrots Vichy (page 218) and Puréed Potatoes (page 213).

Pâté is nothing more than a high-toned word for meat loaf. The French, of course, pride themselves on their pâtés, such as this one made with veal.

On a somewhat lesser plane, they take credit for what is known as gâteau de viande, or meat cake. This makes a fine luncheon dish.

Perhaps the ultimate ground-veal dish in the entire French repertoire is quenelles of veal, delicate ovals of forcemeat baked in a rich cream sauce of various flavors. The one that follows is called belle aurore, or "beautiful dawn," thus named because of the pale-rose color of the sauce. To make this dish, we urge the home cook to use a food processor. An electric blender could be used, but it is less efficient and far more difficult to achieve the proper texture.

Veal Pâté

18 or more servings

1½ pounds coarsely ground veal
1½ pounds calf's liver, cut into 1-inch cubes
1½ pounds coarsely ground lean pork
¾-pound slab of unsalted fatback
¼ pound sliced mushrooms, about 1½ cups
1 clove garlic, thinly sliced
2 shallots, thinly sliced
2 teaspoons Cognac
1 teaspoon chopped fresh thyme or ½ teaspoon dried

½ cup heavy cream
½ teaspoon saltpeter, available in drugstores
¼ teaspoon ground cloves
¼ teaspoon quatre épices (see note) or mace
½ teaspoon nutmeg
¼ cup pistachios
½ pound boiled ham, cut into ½-inch cubes
Salt and freshly ground pepper
1 bay leaf
½ cup Veal Broth (page 197) or chicken broth

1. Preheat the oven to 350 degrees.

2. Prepare the veal, liver, and pork and set aside.

3. Cut half a pound of the fatback into very thin sheets for lining a twelve-cup pâté mold. Line the bottom and sides of the mold with the sheets of fatback, leaving the ends hanging over the sides of the mold.

4. Cut the remaining fatback into small cubes and add them to a heavy skillet. Cook until rendered of fat and starting to brown. Add the mushrooms, garlic, shallots, and Cognac and cook briefly.

5. Add the liver and cook over high heat, stirring, about five minutes. Do not overcook. The liver must remain slightly rare inside or it will dry out.

6. Empty the liver-and-mushroom mixture into the container of a food processor or blender. Add the thyme and blend to a paste. If using a blender, this will have to be done in several steps.

7. Spoon and scrape this mixture into a mixing bowl. Add the veal and pork to the liver mixture.

8. Add the cream, saltpeter, cloves, quatre épices, nutmeg, pistachios, ham, salt, and pepper. Blend well. If you wish to test the mixture for seasonings, cook a small amount in a skillet until well done. Taste and add seasonings as desired.

9. Spoon and scrape the mixture into the prepared mold. Smooth over the top. Place one bay leaf in the center of the pâté. Bring over the edges of the pieces of fatback that hang over the sides of the mold. Add more fatback as necessary so that the pâté is totally enclosed. Cover with the lid of the mold.

10. Set the mold in a shallow baking dish and pour boiling water around it. Place in the oven and bake one hour and forty-five minutes. Add the veal broth.

11. Let the pâté stand at room temperature for an hour. Do not pour off the fat from around the pâté. Cover with a board cut to fit inside the mold. Add a heavy weight (about three pounds) and let stand until it reaches room temperature. Refrigerate.

12. To serve, unmold and scrape off and discard the fat. Serve sliced.

NOTE: Quatre épices can be bought in fine specialty food shops. It is a mixture of white pepper, grated nutmeg, ground ginger, and powdered cloves in the proportions 12-3-2-1, approximately.

Gâteau de Viande

(French meat loaf)

6 to 10 servings

2 tablespoons butter
2 tablespoons finely chopped shallots
2 tablespoons chopped onion
½ teaspoon finely minced garlic
¼ pound mushrooms, finely diced, about 1½ cups
Salt and freshly ground pepper to taste

½ cup crushed fresh or canned tomatoes
2 pounds ground veal
¾ pound fresh chicken livers
1 cup fine fresh bread crumbs
2 eggs
3 tablespoons finely chopped parsley

1. Preheat the oven to 400 degrees.
2. Melt the butter in a saucepan and, when it is hot, add the shallots, onion, and garlic. Cook about five minutes, stirring. Add the mushrooms, salt, and pepper. Cook, stirring frequently, about eight minutes. Add the tomatoes and cook about ten minutes. Let cool.
3. Place the veal in a mixing bowl and add the onion-and-tomato mixture.

4. Chop the chicken livers until fine (blending would make them too fine). Add them to the meat mixture. Add the remaining ingredients plus salt and pepper to taste.

5. Spoon the mixture into a loaf pan measuring about 9 x 5 x 3 inches. Set the pan in a larger heatproof dish and pour boiling water around it. Cover lightly with foil and bake one hour. Remove the foil and bake thirty minutes longer. Serve hot with tomato sauce or cold as an appetizer.

Quenelles de Veau Belle Aurore
(Veal dumplings with tomato and cream sauce)

About 18 quenelles

1 pound very lean veal, free of
    fat and gristle
1 large egg yolk
Salt and freshly ground pepper
    to taste
1/8 teaspoon freshly grated nut-
    meg

1½ cups heavy cream
Sauce Belle Aurore (page 205)
1 small truffle, coarsely chopped
    (optional)

1. Cut the meat into one-inch cubes and put into the container of a food processor. With the lid off, add the egg yolk, salt, pepper, and nutmeg. Stir the ingredients with a wooden spatula.

2. Put the lid on and process the ingredients, gradually adding the cream. Scrape the mixture into another bowl. Test for seasonings by dropping a small spoonful into simmering water and tasting.

3. Chill for thirty minutes or longer. The colder the mixture, the easier it will be to shape it into quenelles.

4. Butter a flameproof cooking utensil large enough to hold the quenelles (we use an oval baking dish that measures 10 x 16 x 2 inches).

5. To shape the quenelles, have ready two large soup spoons and a bowl filled with very hot water.

6. Hold one spoon in the right hand and scoop up a heaping amount of mixture. Transfer the spoon to the left hand. Dip the second spoon in the hot water and smooth the top of the mixture. Quickly scoop the rounded mixture out of the spoon to make a neat, egg-shaped quenelle. Transfer to the baking dish. Continue making quenelles, arranging them close together and barely touching.

7. Cover the quenelles with a piece of buttered wax paper cut to fit inside the baking dish.

8. Meanwhile, bring six cups of water and one tablespoon of salt to the boil. Gradually ladle enough of this liquid onto the wax paper, letting it seep over the edges and surround the quenelles, to barely cover the quenelles.

9. Place the quenelles over moderate heat and bring to the boil, gently shaking the baking dish so that the quenelles do not stick.

10. Poach the quenelles about four minutes. Lift up the paper and, using a rubber spatula, gently turn the quenelles. Replace the paper and cook about five minutes longer. Using a slotted spoon, remove the quenelles and drain them on paper towels.

11. Arrange them on a hot platter and spoon the sauce over. Garnish, if desired, with truffles.

12. Serve with Buttered Fine Noodles (page 209).

Rigatoni al Forno

(Rigatoni in a meat and tomato sauce)

8 to 12 servings

7 tablespoons butter
2 cups finely chopped onion
1 pound mushrooms
½ pound ground veal
½ pound Italian sausages
1 teaspoon finely minced garlic
1 tablespoon finely chopped
  fresh basil or 1 teaspoon
  dried
¾ teaspoon crushed sage
¾ teaspoon crushed oregano
1 dried red pepper, chopped
  (optional)
6 cups canned, peeled Italian
  plum tomatoes

Salt and freshly ground pepper
  to taste
1 cup water
1 cup Veal Broth (page 197) or
  chicken broth
¼ cup finely chopped parsley
2 tablespoons olive oil
1 pound rigatoni or ziti
½ pound mozzarella cheese, cut
  into ½-inch cubes
2 cups freshly grated Parmesan
  cheese

1. Heat three tablespoons of butter in a heavy skillet and add the onion. Cook, stirring, until wilted.

2. If the mushrooms are tiny, leave them whole. Otherwise, quarter them or slice them, depending on size. Add the mushrooms to the onion and cook, stirring frequently, until the mushrooms give up their liquid. Cook further until the liquid evaporates.

3. In a separate skillet, cook the veal and sausage meat (pull off the sausage skins) until the meat has rendered its fat. Pour off the fat. Add the meat to the mushroom mixture and stir it in. Sprinkle with garlic,

basil, sage, oregano, and red pepper. Cook about three minutes, stirring. Add the tomatoes, salt, pepper, water, and broth. Simmer one hour, stirring frequently.

4. Add the chopped parsley and simmer fifteen minutes. Stir in the olive oil and set aside to cool.

5. Drop the rigatoni into a large quantity of boiling salted water and cook, stirring rapidly to make certain that the pieces of pasta float freely and do not stick to the bottom. Cook about eight minutes. Do not cook longer, for the pasta will be baked. Immediately drain the pasta into a colander and run cold water over it. Drain well.

6. Preheat the oven to 400 degrees.

7. Spoon a thin layer of sauce into a baking dish 13½ x 1¾ x 8¾ inches. Add a single layer of rigatoni, scatter over it half the mozzarella, and sprinkle with a tablespoon or so of Parmesan cheese. Continue making layers of sauce, pasta, mozzarella, and Parmesan, ending with a layer of sauce and Parmesan. Use only about half a cup of the Parmesan for the dish. The rest will be served on the side.

8. Dot the casserole with the remaining butter and bake, uncovered, for thirty minutes, or until bubbling hot throughout. Run the dish briefly under the broiler to give it a nice brown glaze. Serve the dish cut into squares with Parmesan cheese on the side.

9. Serve with a tossed green salad.

According to the late Princess Alexandra Kropotkin, there was once a tavern in the Russian town of Torjok, situated between Moscow and St. Petersburg. And the owner of the tavern was named Pojarski. If the dishes that bear his name today are an index of his talents, he must have been an extraordinary chef and host. The specialties of the house of Pojarski were ground-meat dishes.

Côtelettes de Veau Pojarski
(Breaded veal "cutlets")

4 servings

1 pound lean veal
⅛ teaspoon ground nutmeg
Salt and freshly ground pepper
    to taste
1 cup heavy cream

1½ cups fine fresh bread
    crumbs
5 tablespoons butter
Lemon wedges

1. Have the veal twice ground by the butcher. Or use a food processor to give the texture of twice-ground veal

2. Chill the veal and chill a mixing bowl. Both should be very cold.

3. Place the veal in the mixing bowl and add the nutmeg, salt, pepper, cream, and three-quarters cup of the bread crumbs. Blend well, beating briskly in a circular fashion with a wooden spoon. Or you could continue making this in a food processor.

4. Divide the mixture into four equal portions. Shape into patties, roll in bread crumbs to coat all over, then shape into a cutlet to resemble a veal chop with bone.

5. Heat two tablespoons of the butter in a heavy skillet and add the veal "chops." Brown on one side about five minutes and turn. Continue cooking and browning on the other side, about seven minutes, or until the meat is cooked through without becoming dry.

6. Heat three tablespoons of butter in a heavy skillet. When it melts, swirl the skillet until butter is foamy. Continue cooking until butter is hazelnut-colored. Pour over the veal and garnish with lemon wedges.

7. Serve with Endives au Gratin (page 219).

Boulettes de Veau Stroganoff

(Veal meat balls Stroganoff)

4 to 6 servings

1 pound ground veal
1 egg, lightly beaten
⅓ cup fine fresh bread crumbs
¼ cup milk
¼ teaspoon grated nutmeg
Salt and freshly ground pepper
  to taste
3 teaspoons paprika
4 tablespoons butter

¼ pound mushrooms, thinly
  sliced
⅓ cup finely chopped onion
¼ cup dry sherry
2 tablespoons Demi-glace (page
  197) or canned beef gravy
¼ cup heavy cream
1 cup sour cream
¼ cup finely chopped parsley

1. Place the meat in a mixing bowl and add the egg.

2. Soak the crumbs in milk and add this to the meat. Add the nutmeg, salt, and pepper and mix well with the hands. Shape the mixture into balls about one and one-half inches in diameter. There should be about forty meat balls.

3. Sprinkle a pan with the paprika and roll the meat balls in it.

4. Heat the butter in a heavy skillet and cook the meat balls, turning gently, until they are nicely browned, about five minutes. Sprinkle the mushrooms and onions between and around the meat balls and shake the skillet to distribute the ingredients evenly. Cook about one minute and partly cover. Simmer about five minutes and add the sherry and

demi-glace. Stir in the heavy cream. Partly cover and cook over low heat about fifteen minutes. Stir in the sour cream and bring just to the boil. Serve piping hot, sprinkled with parsley.

5. Serve with Buttered Fine Noodles (page 209).

One of the many curious names in cookery is the title Koenigsberger Klopse. It is essentially meat balls in a caper and cream sauce. The name derives from the town of Koenigsberg, halfway between Frankfurt and Bayreuth. Klops is simply the German word for meat ball.

Koenigsberger Klopse
(*Veal balls in sour cream and caper sauce*)

4 to 6 servings

¾ pound ground veal
½ pound ground pork
Salt and freshly ground pepper
   to taste
5 tablespoons butter
½ cup finely chopped onion
½ English muffin or hard roll
1 egg, lightly beaten
½ cup chopped parsley
1 teaspoon anchovy paste
½ teaspoon grated lemon rind
   (optional)
⅛ teaspoon grated nutmeg

¼ cup flour
2½ cups Veal Broth (page 197)
   or chicken broth
½ cup white Rhine or Moselle
   wine
½ cup sour cream
1 egg yolk
⅓ cup drained capers
1 tablespoon imported mustard,
   such as Dijon or Düsseldorf
Juice of ½ lemon or more to
   taste

1. In a mixing bowl, combine the veal, pork, salt, and pepper.

2. Heat one tablespoon of butter in a small skillet and cook the onion until wilted. Remove from the heat and let cool slightly.

3. Meanwhile, put the English muffin half in a small bowl and add about one-half cup of water. Let stand until water is absorbed.

4. To the meat in the mixing bowl, add the egg and the cooked onion. Squeeze the muffin half to extract most of the moisture. Tear it into small pieces and add it to the meat.

5. Add half the parsley, anchovy paste, lemon rind, and nutmeg. Blend well with the fingers.

6. Shape the mixture into twelve or fourteen balls.

7. Heat the remaining four tablespoons of butter in a saucepan and add the flour, stirring with a whisk. When blended, add the broth, stirring rapidly with the whisk. When blended and smooth, add the wine and salt and pepper to taste.

8. Add the meatballs one by one to the sauce. Let cook twenty-five minutes, stirring gently and shaking the pan to prevent sticking.

9. Blend the sour cream, egg yolk, capers, mustard, and lemon juice.

10. Remove the balls from the sauce and add the sour-cream mixture, stirring. Cook gently until sauce starts to simmer. Add the meatballs and serve immediately.

11. Serve with Buttered Fine Noodles (page 209).

This recipe is from the Italian Pavillion in New York.

Veal Primavera

(Veal patties with fresh tomato sauce)

6 servings

2 pounds ground veal	6 tablespoons butter
2 eggs, lightly beaten	1 cup dry white wine
1 tablespoon finely chopped parsley	½ cup Demi-glace (page 197) or canned beef gravy
6 tablespoons freshly grated Parmesan cheese	½ pound thinly sliced prosciutto
1 teaspoon Worcestershire sauce	½ pound thinly sliced Gruyère or Swiss cheese
Salt and freshly ground pepper to taste	3 cups Primavera Sauce (page 204)
Flour for dredging	

1. Place the veal in a mixing bowl. Add the eggs, parsley, Parmesan cheese, Worcestershire sauce, salt, and pepper and blend well. Shape into eighteen portions and flatten each into a patty.

2. Dredge the patties lightly in flour. Shake off excess.

3. Melt the butter in a large skillet and cook the patties on both sides until golden brown, about three minutes to a side.

4. Add the wine and cook over high heat until the liquid almost completely disappears. Add the demi-glace and bring to the boil.

5. Cover each patty with one slice of prosciutto, folded over if necessary so that it fits. Cover each with a slice of cheese, also folded over if necessary. Cover the skillet and cook about five minutes, or until cheese is melted.

6. Serve with Buttered Fine Noodles (page 209) and Primavera Sauce spooned over, or on the side.

No other part of the world has a greater sophistication with ground veal than Scandinavia. Swedish meat patties with dill sauce, Swedish meat balls, and an inspired creation called *Wallenbergare,* a specialty of the Operakällaren in Stockholm, are distinguished examples.

Swedish Meat Patties with Dill Sauce

4 to 8 servings

1 pound ground veal
6 tablespoons bread crumbs
1½ cups heavy cream
⅛ teaspoon nutmeg
Salt and freshly ground pepper
   to taste

3 tablespoons butter
2 tablespoons finely chopped
   onion
¼ cup dry white wine
2 tablespoons finely chopped
   dill

1. Combine the meat and bread crumbs in a mixing bowl. Add one cup of heavy cream, the nutmeg, salt and pepper, and mix until thoroughly blended.

2. Shape the mixture into eight balls and, using moistened fingers, flatten and shape the balls like hamburgers.

3. Melt the butter in a heavy skillet and, when it is hot, add the patties. Cook about three minutes to the side, or to any desired degree of doneness. Remove from the skillet and keep warm.

4. Add the onion to the fat in the skillet and cook, stirring, until wilted. Add the wine and cook until it is almost totally reduced. Add the remaining half cup of cream and cook over high heat until it is slightly reduced, about three minutes. Stir in the chopped dill.

5. Return the patties to the sauce and cook, turning, until heated through. Serve with the sauce.

6. Serve with Puréed Potatoes (page 213).

This recipe is from the Operakällaren restaurant in Stockholm.

Wallenbergare

(Vealburgers Swedish-style)

4 servings

1 pound ground veal
Salt and freshly ground pepper
   to taste
¼ teaspoon grated nutmeg
4 large egg yolks

¾ cup heavy cream
1 cup fine fresh bread crumbs
2 tablespoons butter
1 tablespoon peanut, vegetable,
   or corn oil

1. Put the veal in a large mixing bowl and add salt, pepper, nutmeg, and egg yolks. Beat with a wooden spoon to blend.

2. Add the cream gradually, beating vigorously and constantly with the spoon. Place the bowl in the refrigerator or, better, the freezer and chill thoroughly. Do not freeze. The mixture should be cold enough to shape.

3. Shape the mixture into four or eight portions. Flatten into sausage-shaped patties and coat all over with bread crumbs. Pat lightly to help crumbs adhere. Chill until ready to cook.

4. Heat the butter and the oil and add the patties. Cook until golden brown on one side, about five minutes. Turn and cook about five minutes on the other side until golden and cooked through.

5. Serve with lingonberry jam, green peas, and Puréed Potatoes (page 213).

Swedish Meat Balls

6 to 8 servings

1 pound ground round steak
½ pound ground veal
½ pound ground pork
3 tablespoons finely chopped
   parsley
1 cup fine bread crumbs
1½ cups heavy cream
2 eggs
Salt and freshly ground pepper
   to taste

¼ teaspoon nutmeg
4 tablespoons butter
3 tablespoons chopped onion
1 tablespoon paprika
2 tablespoons flour
1½ cups Veal Broth (page 197)
   or chicken broth
2 cups sour cream

1. In a mixing bowl, combine the beef, veal, and pork. Add the parsley, bread crumbs, one cup of the cream, eggs, salt, pepper, and nutmeg. Blend well with the fingers.

2. Lightly oil a platter to hold the meat balls. Shape the meat into approximately forty-eight balls. Dipping the fingers in cold water will facilitate the shaping.

3. Heat the butter in one or two large skillets and add the meat balls. Cook about three minutes on one side and turn. Cook, shaking the skillet and turning the balls, five to ten minutes. Do not overcook or they become dry.

4. Remove the meat balls and keep them warm. To the skillet, add the onion and cook, stirring, until wilted. Add the paprika and flour, stirring. Add one cup of veal broth and stir until blended and smooth. Cook, stirring, about two minutes.

5. Add the sour cream and bring to the boil, stirring. Blend the remaining broth with remaining heavy cream and stir it in. Bring to the boil. Add the meat balls and heat thoroughly.

6. Serve with Puréed Potatoes (page 213).

This is a dish with which we began a memorable meal in the seaport town of Genoa about two years ago. It consists of veal balls wrapped in lettuce. The lettuce packages are cooked briefly in broth and served hot with grated Parmesan cheese. It could be called a soup, but in any event makes an excellent first course.

Lattughe Ripiene in Brodo
(Stuffed lettuce in broth)

4 servings

2 large heads Boston lettuce
1 pound ground lean veal
4 tablespoons finely chopped
  onion
1 small clove garlic, finely
  minced
¼ teaspoon freshly grated nutmeg

1 egg, lightly beaten
Salt and freshly ground pepper
  to taste
¼ cup finely chopped parsley
2 cups Veal Broth (page 197) or
  chicken broth
½ cup freshly grated Parmesan
  cheese

1. Remove the large outer leaves of the lettuce. There should be about twenty-four leaves. Reserve the inner leaves for use in salads.

2. Add the leaves to a kettle of boiling salted water. Let the water return to the boil and drain the lettuce. Dry on paper towels, taking care not to break the leaves.

3. Blend the veal, onion, garlic, nutmeg, egg, salt, pepper, and parsley in a mixing bowl and mix well with the hands or a wooden spoon.

4. Lay out the lettuce leaves and sprinkle with salt and pepper.

5. Shape the mixture into approximately twenty-four balls and add one ball to the center of each leaf. Carefully fold over the leaves to enclose the meat balls, envelope fashion. Arrange the stuffed lettuce in one layer in a casserole and add the broth. Cover and bring to the boil. Simmer about ten minutes, or until meat is cooked. Serve in soup bowls with a little broth in each. Serve grated cheese on the side.

In any list of America's favorite foods there would, of course, be hamburgers, hot dogs, and fried chicken. The American appetite is equally voracious for that specialty known variously as chili con carne, plain chili, or "a bowl of red." An all-American version of chili—called Kansas City chili—follows. There is also a recipe for a cousin to the chili dish that is called picadillo, another spicy ground-meat specialty, this one from San Antonio.

Kansas City Chili

6 to 8 servings

2 tablespoons fat, preferably rendered suet, or use peanut, vegetable, or corn oil
2 pounds ground veal
1 tablespoon finely minced garlic
¼ cup chili powder
2 teaspoons cumin seeds
2 teaspoons oregano
¼ teaspoon ground cloves
Salt and freshly ground pepper to taste
1 bay leaf
3 cups canned tomatoes with tomato paste
½ to 1 cup Veal Broth (page 197) or chicken broth

1. Heat the fat in a skillet and add the meat. Cook, stirring with a wooden spoon to break up the lumps.

2. Add the garlic and chili powder. Crush or grind the cumin seeds and oregano and add. Add the cloves, salt, and pepper. Cook, stirring briefly, and add the bay leaf and tomatoes. Stir to blend. Simmer forty-five minutes.

3. Tilt the pan and skim off most of the fat from the surface. Add veal broth to obtain the desired consistency.

4. Serve piping hot with Baked Rice (page 211).

NOTE: Many people, of course, don't think chili exists without onions and green peppers. If you are among those, cook four cups of chopped onion and one cup of chopped green pepper in the fat before adding the meat.

San Antonio Picadillo

6 to 8 servings

½ pound ground veal
½ pound ground pork
½ to ¾ cup water
1 cup red, ripe, fresh or canned, peeled tomatoes
Salt and freshly ground pepper to taste
½ pound potatoes
1 teaspoon chopped garlic, more or less to taste

1 6-ounce can tomato paste
¾ cup diced pimentos
½ teaspoon crushed oregano
2 to 4 canned jalapeño peppers, available in specialty food shops
1 or 2 tablespoons jalapeño pepper liquid from the can
¾ cup toasted almonds

1. Place the veal and pork in a saucepan and add just enough water to cover. Bring to the boil and break up the lumps with the side of a kitchen spoon. Cover and let simmer thirty minutes.

2. Add the tomatoes, salt, and pepper.

3. Peel the potatoes and cut them into half-inch cubes. Add the potatoes to the saucepan. Add the garlic, tomato paste, pimentos, and oregano. Split the jalapeño peppers in half and remove and discard the seeds. Dice or thinly slice the peppers and add them. Add the pepper liquid and cover. Cook fifteen minutes, or until the potatoes are tender. Add the toasted almonds.

4. Serve in individual bowls with tortilla chips on the side.

Zucchini Ripieni

(Zucchini stuffed with veal and pine nuts)

6 servings

3 zucchini, about 1½ pounds
2 tablespoons olive oil
¼ cup finely chopped onion
1 clove garlic, finely minced
6 tablespoons finely chopped green pepper
Salt and freshly ground pepper to taste
1 teaspoon oregano

½ pound ground veal
¼ cup pine nuts
1 egg
6 tablespoons fine fresh bread crumbs
2 tablespoons freshly grated Parmesan cheese
Tomato Sauce I (page 203)

1. Split the zucchini in half lengthwise. Using a spoon or melon-ball cutter, scoop out the center flesh, leaving a shell about one-quarter inch thick. There should be about one cup of pulp.

2. Drop the shells into cold water and bring to the boil. Simmer thirty seconds, drain, and run under cold running water. Drain well.

3. In a skillet, heat half the oil and cook the onion, garlic, green pepper, and zucchini pulp until onion is wilted. Add salt, pepper, and oregano. Remove from the heat and cool briefly. Stir in the veal, pine nuts, egg, and four tablespoons of bread crumbs. Blend well with the hands. Stuff the squash shells with the mixture and place in a baking dish. Sprinkle with salt and pepper. Blend the remaining bread crumbs and cheese and sprinkle over the stuffed zucchini. Dribble the remaining oil over all.

4. When ready to cook, preheat the oven to 400 degrees. Bake the zucchini uncovered for thirty minutes.

5. Serve with Tomato Sauce I (page 203) and Buttered Fine Noodles (page 209).

Veal Stuffing

(For a 12- to 14-pound goose or turkey)

1 pound ground veal	Salt and freshly ground pepper
1½ pounds ground pork (there	to taste
should be about two parts	1 cup finely chopped parsley
lean pork to one part pork fat)	6 tablespoons whole blanched
1 goose or turkey liver	pistachio nuts
3 tablespoons butter, chicken	¼ cup chopped black truffles
fat, goose fat, or bacon fat	(optional)
2 cups finely chopped onion	1 3¾-ounce jar or container foie
1 tablespoon finely chopped gar-	gras, cut into cubes (optional)
lic	2 eggs, lightly beaten
2 teaspoons chopped fresh basil	2 cups bread crumbs
or 1 teaspoon dried	2 tablespoons Cognac
1 tablespoon chopped dried	
sage	

1. Prepare the veal and pork in separate batches and set aside. Chop the goose or turkey liver.

2. Heat the butter in a skillet and add the onion and garlic. Cook until wilted and add the pork, stirring to break up any lumps. Add the basil and sage. Add the chopped liver and veal, stirring to break up lumps. Stir until the meat loses its red color. Add salt and pepper to taste and the parsley. Blend well.

3. Scrape the mixture into a large mixing bowl and add the remaining ingredients.

4. Use the mixture to stuff a twelve- to fourteen-pound goose or turkey.

•Odd Parts•

There are many people in this world who will consider this the choicest and most vital section of this book. They are people of unfailing taste and appetite who know that these are among the most delectable parts of veal. We think the name "odd parts" is the most all-embracing and acceptable, but they go by various names—variety cuts, innards, offal (British), *abats* (French), *frattaglie* (Italian).

We find it absolutely irresistible in discussing the various meats in the category—liver, brains, sweetbreads, heart, tongue, head, kidney, feet—to quote one of our favorite lines from the *Wise Encyclopedia of Cookery*. The author's name is not attributed, but we believe it to have been the celebrated American gourmet known as Lucius Beebe.

The author was referring only to tripe. We will alter the quotation to our own advantage and let it read as follows: The odd parts of the animal, "like certain alluring vices," are "enjoyed by societies to extreme, the topmost and the lowermost strata, while the multitudinous middle classes of the world look upon [them] with genteel disdain and noses tilted. Patricians relished [these morsels] in Babylon's gardens, plebeians have always welcomed [them] as something good and cheap, and always the peasant cook has taught the prince how to eat [them]." That is the lesson for the day.

BRAINS

If the odd parts of veal are the choicest parts of the animal, the brains are
to many fine palates choicest of them all. They do have a texture and
flavor of such a special nature it is difficult to compare them to a better-
known quantity.

The variety of brain dishes seems to be limitless. First off, they are
cooked briefly in salted water, with a trace of vinegar, bay leaf, thyme,
and peppercorns. After poaching, they are then ready perhaps to be
cooked *au beurre noir*—with brown butter. Or they may be simply sliced
and served cold with a vinaigrette sauce. They may be served with a garnish of asparagus, or perhaps a garnish of spinach.

How to prepare brains prior to further cooking

Calf's brains	1 bay leaf
2 cups cold water	1 sprig fresh thyme or ½ tea-
Salt to taste	spoon dried
2 tablespoons white vinegar	6 peppercorns

1. Soak the brains in cold water to cover for several hours. Drain.

2. Pick over the brains. Remove and discard all the fiberlike threads
and membranes. The white connecting tissues and all the pink fleshy
portions are edible.

3. Place the brains in a saucepan and add the remaining ingredients.
Bring to the boil and simmer about one minute. Remove from the heat
and let stand.

Cervelle de Veau Florentine

(Brains on a bed of spinach)

4 to 6 servings

3 sets calf's brains
2 pounds, or 2 10-ounce pack-
    ages, fresh spinach
4 tablespoons butter
3 tablespoons flour
2 cups milk
Salt and freshly ground pepper to
    taste

⅛ teaspoon nutmeg
Dash of Tabasco
½ cup heavy cream
2 egg yolks
¼ cup grated Parmesan cheese

1. Prepare the brains (page 149) and set them aside.

2. Preheat the oven to 400 degrees.

3. Drop the spinach into boiling water to cover. When the water returns to the boil, let simmer about five minutes. Drain well. Run under cold water to cool. Squeeze to extract most of the moisture. Chop the spinach and set aside.

4. Melt half the butter in a saucepan and add the flour, stirring with a wire whisk. Add the milk, stirring rapidly with the whisk. When the mixture is thickened and smooth, add salt, pepper, nutmeg, and Tabasco. Cook about ten minutes, stirring often with the whisk.

5. Add the cream and blend well. Add the yolks, stirring rapidly. Cook about fifteen seconds and remove from the heat.

6. Heat the remaining butter and add the spinach. Cook, tossing and stirring until heated through.

7. Spoon the spinach onto a baking dish and smooth it over. Cut each portion of brain in half and arrange the pieces, cut side up, over the spinach. Spoon the sauce over and smooth it. Sprinkle with cheese and bake twenty minutes, or until piping hot and lightly browned on top.

8. Serve with boiled parsleyed potatoes.

Veal Meat Loaf with Herbs

Escalopes de Veau Holstein

Longe de Veau Farcie

Côtes de Veau Belles des Bois

Escalopes de Veau Viennoise

Rognons de Veau Ardennaise

Ris de Veau aux Petits Pois

Veal Chili with Olives and Peppers

Vitello Tonnato

Paillarde of Veal

Escalopes de Veau aux Champignons

Rouelles de Veau à la Savoyarde

Paula Peck's Veal Rollatine

Poitrine de Veau Farcie aux Epinards

Cervelle de Veau
au Beurre Noir

(Calf's brains with brown butter)

2 servings

1 pound calf's brains	2 tablespoons finely chopped
Salt and freshly ground pepper	parsley
to taste	2 tablespoons capers, drained
Flour for dredging	2 teaspoons red wine vinegar
4 tablespoons butter	

1. Prepare the brains (page 149). Split them in half lengthwise.

2. Season with salt and pepper and coat lightly with flour.

3. Melt half the butter in a heavy skillet. Add the brains and cook on one side over moderate heat until golden brown, about five minutes. Turn the brains and cook about two minutes on the other side.

4. Transfer the brains to two warm plates and sprinkle with parsley. Add the remaining butter to the skillet with its drippings and cook until quite brown, stirring. Do not burn the butter. Immediately add the capers and wine vinegar and spoon equal portions of the sauce over each serving.

5. Serve with boiled parsleyed potatoes.

Cervelle de Veau
Maréchale

(Breaded calf's brains with asparagus)

6 servings

3 or 4 sets calf's brains, 1¼ to	2 cups fine fresh bread crumbs
1¾ pounds	¼ cup peanut, vegetable, or
½ cup flour	corn oil
2 eggs	6 tablespoons butter
3 tablespoons olive oil	18 asparagus tips, each about 4
¼ cup water	inches long
Salt and freshly ground pepper	6 to 10 thin black-truffle slices
to taste	(optional)

1. Prepare the brains (see page 149).

2. Dredge the portions of brains in flour. Shake off excess.

3. Beat the eggs with oil, water, salt, and pepper. Dip the pieces of brain in egg, then in bread crumbs.

4. Heat the oil and two tablespoons of butter in a large skillet and add the breaded brains. Cook about five minutes, or until golden brown on one side. Turn and cook until golden on the other.

5. Place the asparagus tips in a skillet and add cold water to cover and salt to taste. Bring to the boil and simmer thirty seconds. Drain.

6. Transfer the pieces of brains to a hot platter and garnish between the pieces with asparagus tips. Cover each piece with a slice of truffle. Heat the remaining butter until foamy and pour over all.

7. Serve with Skillet Potatoes (page 214).

Cervelle de Veau Vinaigrette

(Calf's brains vinaigrette)

8 or more servings

2 sets calf's brains
1 hard-cooked egg, chopped
1 tablespoon drained capers
2 tablespoons finely chopped
  onion
2 tablespoons finely chopped
  parsley
Juice of half a lemon

1 tablespoon vinegar
4 tablespoons peanut, vegetable,
  or corn oil
1 tablespoon imported prepared
  mustard, such as Dijon or
  Düsseldorf
Salt and freshly ground pepper
  to taste

1. Prepare the brains (see page 149). Cut each set of brains in half. Cut each half into six pieces of equal size. Arrange in a serving dish.

2. Sprinkle with chopped egg, capers, onion, and parsley.

3. Blend the remaining ingredients in a bowl and beat well with a whisk. Pour the sauce over the brains and serve cold or at room temperature.

This recipe is from the Four Seasons in New York.

A Salad of Calf's Brains and Winter Greens

6 to 8 servings

1½ calf's brains, about 1¼ pounds
1 head Belgian endive, trimmed and cut into bite-size pieces
2 cups loosely packed spinach cut into bite-size pieces
1 cup loosely packed watercress sprigs, with stems removed
1 cup limestone lettuce cut into bite-size pieces
1 cup chicory cut into bite-size pieces
1 cup escarole cut into bite-size pieces
1 cup heart of romaine cut into bite-size pieces
1 cup "red" or "leaf" lettuce cut into bite-size pieces
¼ cup loosely packed fresh coriander leaves
¼ cup loosely packed fresh chervil leaves (optional)
2 egg yolks
4 tablespoons imported pre-pared mustard, preferably Maille brand with three herbs (see note)
2 cups fine fresh bread crumbs
Salt and freshly ground pepper to taste
3 tablespoons walnut oil (see note)
2 tablespoons wine vinegar, preferably sherry wine vinegar (see note)
3 tablespoons olive oil
1 teaspoon tarragon vinegar
½ cup peanut, vegetable, or corn oil
½ cup well-drained capers
4 tablespoons butter
½ cup carrots cut into the finest possible shreds (optional)
½ cup white part of leek cut into the finest possible shreds (optional)
1 truffle, thinly sliced (optional)

1. Place the brains in a mixing bowl and add cold water to cover. Let them stand several hours, changing the water frequently. Drain and pick over to the brains to remove the outer membranes, the blood, and other extraneous matter.

2. All the greens should be rinsed well in cold water and well drained.

3. Combine the egg yolks and three tablespoons of mustard in a mixing bowl and beat with a whisk to blend.

4. Cut the brains into one-and-one-half-inch cubes and add to the mustard mixture. Stir to coat.

5. Spread half the crumbs over the bottom of a pan and add the pieces of brain. Sprinkle with remaining crumbs. Gently roll the brain pieces in crumbs to coat thoroughly. Remove the breaded pieces and set aside.

6. To prepare the salad dressing, put one tablespoon of mustard in a mixing bowl and add salt and pepper to taste. Add the walnut oil gradu-

ally, beating rapidly with a whisk. Beat in the wine vinegar, olive oil, and tarragon vinegar.

7. Heat the peanut oil in a skillet and add the capers. Cook, stirring, about two minutes and drain well.

8. Heat the butter in a skillet and add the breaded pieces of brain. Cook about two minutes to a side. The brains should be nicely browned.

9. Put the salad greens in a large bowl and toss with the dressing.

10. Arrange the greens on one large serving dish and arrange the brains over them. Sprinkle with the capers. Scatter the shredded carrots and leek over all and garnish with truffle slices.

NOTE: These ingredients are available where fine specialty foods are sold.

SWEETBREADS

If anyone were to list the ten most basic items for stylish, classic French cooking, veal sweetbreads would inevitably be included.

The anatomical aspects of certain foods are oftentimes best ignored, but as a matter of record sweetbreads are the thymus gland or the pancreas of the calf. It consists of two parts that are attached—one small, the other large—and with the same delectable taste and texture.

Like brains, sweetbreads must first be poached gently in seasoned water before a final cooking. One of the essentials of proper sweetbread cookery is that they be weighted properly after the initial cooking and as they cool. This gives them a finer, firmer texture. Otherwise, they seem puffy and rubbery.

Their uses thereafter are almost poetic: au champagne, au porto, Eugénie, with fettuccine, and so on.

Sweetbreads, in short, have all the class of sterling silver and candlelight.

How to prepare sweetbreads prior to further cooking

1. Pull or pare off and discard any tough membranes from the sweetbreads. Place them in a basin of cold water and refrigerate several hours. Drain and put them in a saucepan and add cold water to cover. Add salt to taste and bring to the boil. Simmer for five minutes. Drain and immediately run under cold running water.

2. Weight down the sweetbreads, to improve their texture: Place them in a deep plate or on a wire rack. Cover with a saucepan or baking dish (depending on the number of sweetbreads). Add weights to the saucepan or baking dish. Refrigerate for at least two hours or overnight.

Ris de Veau Braisés au Porto

(Sweetbreads with port wine sauce)

2 to 4 servings

2 pairs sweetbreads, about 2 pounds
3 tablespoons butter
1 carrot, scraped and cut into rounds
1 onion, peeled and cut into ¼-inch slices
½ cup coarsely sliced celery
6 sprigs fresh parsley
1 clove garlic, peeled
Salt and freshly ground pepper to taste
1 bay leaf

3 sprigs fresh thyme or ½ teaspoon dried
½ cup plus 3 tablespoons port
1 cup Veal Broth (page 197) or chicken broth
1 tablespoon tomato purée
½ pound fresh mushroom caps, quartered, about 3 cups
1 tablespoon finely chopped shallots
1 teaspoon cornstarch
1 tablespoon water

1. Prepare the sweetbreads (see page 155).

2. Heat two tablespoons of butter in a casserole large enough to hold the sweetbreads in one layer. Add the carrot rounds, onion slices, celery, four of the parsley sprigs, garlic, salt and pepper, bay leaf, and thyme. Cook, stirring occasionally, until onion is lightly browned. Arrange the sweetbreads on top.

3. Preheat the oven to 400 degrees.

4. Pour half a cup of port over the sweetbreads. Add the veal broth, two sprigs of parsley, and tomato purée. Cover and bring to the boil.

5. Place the casserole in the oven and bake, basting occasionally, about ten minutes.

6. Remove the dish from the oven. Remove the sweetbreads from the sauce and set aside. Cook the sauce down about five minutes.

7. Heat the remaining tablespoon of butter in a skillet and add the mushrooms, salt, and pepper. Cook until the liquid from the mushrooms evaporates and mushrooms start to brown. Add the shallots and three tablespoons of port. Ignite the port and cook until the flame disappears.

8. Strain the sauce in which the sweetbreads cooked. There should be about one cup. Add this to the mushrooms. Cook about five minutes.

9. Blend the cornstarch and water and stir it into the sauce to thicken. Add the sweetbreads. Return the sweetbreads to the oven, uncovered. Cook, basting once or twice, about ten minutes.

10. Serve with Baked Rice (page 211).

This recipe is from Le Manoir restaurant in New York.

Ris de Veau au Porto Blanc

(Sweetbreads in port)

4 servings

4 pairs sweetbreads, about 3¼ pounds
4 fresh fennel bulbs, about 1¼ pounds
4 tablespoons butter
Salt and freshly ground pepper to taste

½ cup plus two tablespoons port, preferably white port
1 cup heavy cream
1 teaspoon arrowroot or corn- starch
1 teaspoon lemon juice

1. Prepare the sweetbreads (see page 155).

2. Preheat the oven to 350 degrees.

3. Trim the fennel. Quarter the bulbs, then cut into thin strips.

4. Heat the butter in a heavy casserole large enough to hold the sweet-breads in one layer. Add the fennel and cook briefly.

5. Arrange the sweetbreads over the fennel. Sprinkle generously with salt and pepper. Add half a cup of the port and cover. Bring to the boil and place in the oven. Bake forty-five minutes.

6. Remove the sweetbreads to a platter and cover with foil.

7. Strain the fennel but reserve the liquid. There should be about one cup. Using a food processor or food mill, purée the fennel.

8. Cook down the liquid by half over high heat. Add the cream, salt, and pepper and cook about five minutes over high heat.

9. Blend the arrowroot with two tablespoons of port and stir it in. Add the lemon juice. Strain the sauce over the sweetbreads and serve hot with the hot puréed fennel on the side.

Ris de Veau Braisés au Champagne

(Sweetbreads in champagne sauce)

4 servings

2 pairs sweetbreads, about 2
  pounds
2 tablespoons butter
½ cup carrots cut into thin
  rounds
1 small onion, peeled and quartered
½ cup coarsely sliced celery
1 clove garlic, peeled
2 sprigs fresh thyme or ½ teaspoon dried
1 bay leaf
2 sprigs fresh parsley
1 cup Veal Broth (page 197) or
  chicken broth
½ cup champagne
¼ cup dry white wine
1 tablespoon finely chopped
  shallots
1 cup heavy cream

1. Prepare the sweetbreads (see page 155).

2. Melt the butter in a casserole large enough to hold the sweetbreads in one layer. Add the carrot rounds, onion, celery, and garlic. Cook briefly until onions start to take on color. Do not brown.

3. Arrange the sweetbreads on top and add the thyme, bay leaf, and parsley. Add the veal broth and champagne. Cover and cook about thirty minutes.

4. Remove the sweetbreads and keep warm. Strain the broth. There should be about one and one-half cups.

5. Separately, combine the wine and shallots in a saucepan and cook until the liquid is almost completely reduced. Add the strained broth. Cook down to about one-third cup.

6. Add the cream and cook about five minutes over high heat. Add the sweetbreads and cook about fifteen minutes, basting occasionally.

7. Serve with Braised Celery (page 217).

No one knows the precise origin of sweetbreads Eugénie, or sweetbreads Virginia. It is pure conjecture, but reason tells us that the dish was probably created in America by a chef who first served sweetbreads on Virginia ham. Somewhere along the line, some menu maker decided that the dish must be French and thus rechristened it Eugénie.

Sweetbreads Eugénie or Virginia

(Braised sweetbreads on ham)

8 servings

4 pairs sweetbreads, about 4 pounds
4 tablespoons butter
1 cup thinly sliced onion
½ cup sliced carrots
½ cup sliced celery
2 whole cloves garlic, peeled
1 bay leaf
2 sprigs fresh thyme
2 sprigs fresh parsley
Salt and freshly ground pepper

¾ cup dry white wine
¾ cup Veal Broth (page 197) or chicken broth
8 large mushroom caps
6 tablespoons dry sherry
1½ cups heavy cream
8 thin slices raw or cooked ham, preferably country ham or Smithfield
8 slices sandwich bread

1. Prepare the sweetbreads (see page 155).

2. Preheat the oven to 400 degrees.

3. Heat three tablespoons of butter in a baking dish large enough to hold the sweetbreads in one layer. Add the onion, carrots, celery, garlic cloves, bay leaf, thyme, parsley, salt, and pepper. Add the sweetbreads and cover. Cook about ten minutes. Uncover and add the wine and veal broth. Cover and cook five minutes. Transfer the dish to the oven and bake thirty minutes.

4. Uncover and continue baking, basting often, for fifteen minutes. Remove the sweetbreads. Strain the cooking liquid, reserving two cups.

5. Heat one tablespoon of butter and add the mushroom caps. Sprinkle with salt and pepper and cook on high heat until golden brown. Sprinkle with the sherry and strain juices from the mushrooms immediately into a saucepan with the cooking liquids from the sweetbreads.

6. Cook down the liquid to about one-half cup. Add the heavy cream and cook over high heat about five minutes.

7. Arrange the ham slices in one layer in a large casserole. Place the sweetbreads and mushrooms over them and cover. Cook about two minutes. Add the cream sauce and cook, uncovered, until boiling hot.

8. Toast the bread on both sides. Top each slice with a slice of ham, a portion of sweetbreads, and a mushroom cap. Spoon the sauce over all.

9. Serve with Braised Celery (page 217).

Ris de Veau aux Petits Pois

(Braised sweetbreads with green peas)

6 to 8 servings

4 pairs sweetbreads, about 4 pounds
2 carrots, thinly sliced
2 onions, cut into 12 slices
2 ribs celery, cut into ½-inch lengths
2 sprigs fresh thyme or ½ teaspoon dried
1 bay leaf
6 sprigs parsley
Salt and freshly ground pepper
4 tablespoons butter
½ cup dry white wine
½ cup Veal Broth (page 197) or chicken broth
¼ pound lean salt pork
1 cup very small white onions, peeled
2½ cups shelled fresh green peas (or use 2 10-ounce packages frozen peas)
1 teaspoon sugar

1. Prepare the sweetbreads (see page 155).

2. Preheat the oven to 400 degrees.

3. Select a baking dish large enough to hold the sweetbreads in one layer. Rub the bottom with butter and scatter the carrot slices, onion slices, celery, thyme, bay leaf, and parsley over it. Arrange the sweetbreads over the vegetables and sprinkle with salt and pepper. Dot with half the butter. Add the wine and broth. Cover and bring to the boil on top of the stove. Place the dish in the oven and bake thirty minutes.

4. Meanwhile, cut the salt pork into small strips about one inch long and half an inch wide. Place the pieces in a saucepan and add the small onions. Add water to cover. Bring to the boil and simmer one minute. Drain.

5. Return the salt pork and onions to the saucepan and cook, stirring, until pork is rendered of its fat and is golden. Add the remaining two tablespoons of butter, peas, salt, pepper, and sugar. Cover tightly and cook fifteen minutes.

6. When the sweetbreads have baked thirty minutes, uncover and cook, basting occasionally, about thirty minutes longer.

7. Transfer the sweetbreads to a heavy skillet. Strain the liquid from the baking dish over them and discard the vegetables. Add the peas and salt-pork mixture. Cover and cook about five minutes. Uncover and cook about five minutes longer, basting occasionally.

8. Serve with Purée of Celery Root (page 215).

Timbales de Ris de Veau

(Sweetbreads in pastry)

8 to 10 servings

1 pair sweetbreads, about 1
  pound
2 tablespoons butter
⅓ cup chopped carrots
½ cup finely diced onion
1 medium tomato, peeled and
  diced, about ¾ cup
½ tablespoon finely chopped
  garlic
¼ cup finely chopped parsley
⅛ teaspoon dried thyme
2 bay leaves
Salt and freshly ground pepper
  to taste

1 cup Demi-glace (page 197) or
  canned beef gravy
1 pound ground pork
½ pound ground veal
10 shallots, peeled and thinly
  sliced, about ½ cup
2 black truffles, thinly sliced
  (optional)
1 tablespoon finely chopped
  fresh tarragon or ½ teaspoon
  dried
2 tablespoons Calvados or
  Cognac
Pastry made with 3 cups flour

1. Prepare the sweetbreads (see page 155).

2. Preheat the oven to 400 degrees.

3. Cut the sweetbreads into two-inch chunks. Melt the butter in a skillet and add the sweetbreads. Cook, stirring occasionally, about two minutes. Add the carrots, onion, tomato, garlic, parsley, thyme, bay leaves, salt, and pepper. Cook, stirring, about two minutes. Cover with wax paper and place in the oven. Bake ten minutes. Add one-half cup demi-glace and bake about ten minutes longer.

4. Remove the sweetbreads. Put the sauce through a sieve, pushing with the back of a wooden spoon to extract as much liquid as possible from the solids. There should be about one cup. Pour this into a sauce-pan and reduce to one-half cup.

5. Reduce the oven heat to 350 degrees.

6. Put the pork and veal in a mixing bowl and add the shallots, truf-fles, tarragon, salt, pepper, and Calvados. Blend well and add the hot sauce. Stir to blend thoroughly.

7. Roll out the pastry into a round and fit it into an eight-cup round mold, letting the edges overhang. Add one-third of the pork mixture and arrange half the sweetbread pieces over that. Add another third of the pork mixture, the remaining sweetbreads, and a final layer of pork. Pat down and smooth over. Bring the edges of the pastry toward the center, letting the edges overlap slightly (scraps of dough may be rolled and cut into fancy shapes for decoration). Brush with water. If cut-outs of pastry

are used, apply them and brush with water. Cut a small hole in the center to allow steam to escape. Bake one hour and fifteen minutes. Serve with remaining demi-glace.

We came across this recipe purely by chance. To our knowledge, we had never eaten an Italian meal made with curry powder. One rainy night we dined at the Villa d'Este restaurant on Lake Como in Italy and ordered the curried sweetbreads with fettuccine more out of curiosity than anything else. It was one of the most memorable dishes of our visit.

Curried Sweetbreads with Fettuccine

6 to 8 servings

1 pair sweetbreads, about 1½ pounds
1 carrot, trimmed, scraped, and thinly sliced
1 small onion, peeled and thinly sliced
1 clove garlic, finely chopped
6 sprigs parsley
2 sprigs fresh thyme or ½ teaspoon dried
1 bay leaf

2½ cups Veal Broth (page 197) or chicken broth
10 tablespoons butter, at room temperature
½ pound mushrooms, thinly sliced
1 tablespoon curry powder
1 cup heavy cream
1½ pounds fettuccine or linguine
¾ cup grated Parmesan cheese

1. Prepare the sweetbreads (see page 155).

2. Place the sweetbreads in a saucepan and add the carrot, onion, garlic, parsley, thyme, bay leaf, and veal broth. Bring to the boil and simmer five minutes. Drain, but reserve one-half cup of the cooking liquid.

3. When the sweetbreads are cool enough to handle, cut them into half-inch cubes and set aside.

4. Heat two tablespoons of the butter in a saucepan and add the mushrooms. Toss them in the butter until they are wilted and start to brown. Sprinkle with the curry powder and add the reserved half cup of liquid. Simmer about three minutes and add the cubed sweetbreads. Add the cream and bring to the boil. Turn off heat.

5. Cook the fettuccine in boiling salted water to the desired degree of doneness. Drain and place in a large, hot bowl for mixing.

6. Immediately add the remaining butter and the hot sweetbread mixture and toss. Sprinkle with the cheese, toss quickly, and serve piping hot.

LIVER

It is not without reason that calf's liver can be found on the menus of most of the world's great restaurants. The French chef's ways with foie de veau, or calf's liver, are legendary: cooked meunière style, sautéed quickly and served with crisp bacon, sautéed quickly and served with pan butter seasoned with vinegar.

One of the most interesting and unexpected dishes in this book came from a Chinese restaurant in Manhattan. It is thinly sliced liver quickly stir-fried with garlic, green onions, and chilies and served with a spinach garnish.

The key to the proper cooking of calf's liver lies in the word *quickly*. The liver should be cooked over high heat for only a few seconds to each side. There are differences of opinion as to the thickness of the liver before it is cooked, and it is a question of each person to his own taste. Nonetheless, to reach its maximum palatability it should never be overcooked.

The name meunière, which can be translated as "in the style of the miller's wife," simply means that the liver has been dipped in flour before it is sautéed.

Calf's Liver Meunière

4 servings

1 pound calf's liver, cut into 4 to 8 slices
Salt and freshly ground pepper to taste
Flour for dredging
5 tablespoons butter
4 lemon slices
Chopped parsley for garnish

1. Sprinkle the liver with salt and pepper and dredge lightly on all sides in flour, shaking off the excess.

2. Heat a large skillet and, when very hot, add two tablespoons of butter. Add the liver and cook on one side about one minute. Turn and cook two to five minutes longer to the desired degree of doneness. Transfer the slices to a hot platter and garnish with lemon slices. Wipe out the skillet.

3. Quickly add the remaining three tablespoons butter to the skillet and swirl it around over high heat. Continue cooking until foam sub-

sides and the butter starts to brown. Do not burn. Pour the butter over the liver and garnish with chopped parsley.

4. Serve with boiled potatoes.

In French cookery, the term à l'anglaise has a variety of meanings. It might mean simply boiled in water (which could be taken as a bit of a putdown). It sometimes is applied to breaded foods. And in this case it means served with bacon.

Foie de Veau Sauté à l'Anglaise

(Calf's liver with bacon)

4 servings

8 slices lean bacon
1 pound calf's liver, cut into 4 to 8 slices
Salt and freshly ground pepper to taste

Flour for dredging
2 tablespoons peanut, vegetable, or corn oil
4 tablespoons butter
1 teaspoon Worcestershire sauce

1. Cook the bacon, turning as often as necessary until crisp. Drain on paper towels.
2. As the bacon cooks, sprinkle the liver with salt and pepper and dredge in flour, shaking off the excess.
3. Heat the oil in a skillet and, when it is hot, add the liver. Cook until nicely browned on each side, one to two minutes a side.
4. Remove the liver to a warm platter and pour out the cooking oil. Wipe out the skillet and add the butter. Cook until butter starts to brown and add the Worcestershire. Pour the foaming butter over the calf's liver and garnish each serving with slices of crisp bacon.
5. Serve with boiled potatoes.

Foie de Veau Sauté au Vinaigre

(Sautéed calf's liver with vinegar glaze)

4 servings

1 pound calf's liver, cut into 4 to
   8 slices
Salt and freshly ground pepper
   to taste

½ cup flour
8 tablespoons butter
¼ cup finely chopped parsley
¼ cup red wine vinegar

1. Sprinkle the liver with salt and pepper and dredge lightly on all sides in flour, shaking off the excess.

2. Heat half the butter in a heavy skillet and add the liver. Cook on one side about two minutes. Turn and cook about two minutes more. Transfer the liver to a heated platter and sprinkle with the parsley.

3. Add the remaining butter to the skillet and let it brown briefly. Pour this over the liver. Add the vinegar to the skillet and bring to the boil, swirling it around. Pour this over the liver.

4. Serve with Baked Rice (page 211).

Foie de Veau Sauce Madère

(Calf's liver in Madeira sauce)

2 servings

½ pound calf's liver
2 tablespoons butter
2 tablespoons chopped shallots
2 tablespoons Madeira
½ cup Demi-glace (page 197) or
   canned beef gravy

Salt and freshly ground pepper
   to taste
¼ cup peanut, vegetable, or
   corn oil

1. Cut the liver into very fine julienne strips and set aside.

2. Heat half the butter in a saucepan and add the shallots, Madeira, demi-glace, salt, and pepper. Simmer fifteen minutes. Add the remaining tablespoon of butter and swirl it around until blended.

3. Heat the oil in a skillet and, when it is very hot, add the liver. Cook, tossing, about one minute. Drain in a sieve and add the liver to the Madeira sauce. Serve piping hot.

4. Serve with Baked Rice (page 211).

Calf's Liver with Sage

4 to 6 servings

6 thin slices French bread
6 tablespoons butter
¾ cup finely chopped onion
1 pound calf's liver
¼ cup peanut, vegetable, or corn oil

Salt and freshly ground pepper to taste
1 teaspoon ground sage, more or less to taste
2 tablespoons Cognac
Freshly grated Parmesan cheese

1. Preheat the oven to 350 degrees.

2. Brush the bread slices with two tablespoons of the butter, melted, and arrange the slices on a baking sheet. Bake the bread, turning occasionally, until golden brown.

3. Melt two tablespoons of butter in a saucepan and add the onion. Toss and stir, then cover. Cook ten minutes without browning. The onion should be quite soft.

4. Remove any tough veins and arteries from the liver. Slice it into very fine julienne strips.

5. Heat the oil in a skillet and, when it is quite hot, add the liver strips. Sprinkle with salt and pepper and cook over high heat two to three minutes, shaking the skillet and tossing the strips so that they cook on all sides. Drain in a colander.

6. Heat the remaining two tablespoons of butter in a skillet and, when it is hot, add the liver and onions. Sprinkle with sage and cook, stirring, three or four minutes. Sprinkle with Cognac and ignite it.

7. Serve the liver on the toast and sprinkle lightly with Parmesan cheese. If desired, serve more Parmesan cheese on the side.

8. Serve with boiled parsleyed potatoes.

Pilaf de Foie de Veau

(Calf's liver pilaf)

6 or more servings

THE RICE

4 tablespoons butter
⅓ cup finely chopped onion
1 teaspoon finely minced garlic
2 cups rice
3½ cups Veal Broth (page 197)
  or chicken broth

½ bay leaf
Salt and freshly ground pepper
  to taste

THE PILAF FILLING AND SAUCE

¼ pound mushrooms
4 tablespoons butter
Salt and freshly ground pepper
  to taste
½ cup finely chopped onion
½ teaspoon minced garlic
1 cup tomato purée
½ cup dry white wine
1¼ cups Demi-glace (page 197)
  or canned beef gravy

2 sprigs fresh thyme or ½ teaspoon dried
1 bay leaf
2 pounds calf's liver
¾ cup peanut, vegetable, or
  corn oil
1 tablespoon finely chopped
  parsley

1. Preheat the oven to 400 degrees.

2. Melt the four tablespoons of butter in a heavy, heatproof casserole and add the onion, garlic, and rice. Cook briefly, stirring, and add the veal broth, bay leaf, salt, and pepper. Bring to the boil and cover. Place the casserole in the oven and bake exactly twenty minutes. Remove the casserole but leave the oven on.

3. Meanwhile, prepare the pilaf filling and sauce. Rinse the mushrooms in cold water and drain well. Thinly slice them.

4. Heat two tablespoons of the butter in a large saucepan and add the mushrooms, salt, and pepper. Cook, stirring, over high heat about two minutes and add the onion and garlic. Cook, stirring, about one minute and add the tomato purée, wine, and demi-glace. Add the thyme and bay leaf and cook uncovered, stirring frequently, twenty-five to thirty minutes. Swirl in the remaining two tablespoons of butter, salt, and pepper.

5. As the sauce simmers, prepare the liver. Cut off and discard any tough veins and arteries. Slice the liver into very fine julienne strips.

6. Heat a quarter cup of the oil in a skillet and add just enough strips of liver to fit in one layer. Cook over high heat, tossing and stirring. Sprinkle with salt and pepper. Cook three to five minutes and drain well

167

in a colander. Continue cooking, adding more oil as needed, until all the liver is cooked.

7. Put the liver in a saucepan and add one cup of the sauce. Keep remaining sauce hot.

8. Butter a two-quart, ovenproof mold, preferably one with a rounded bottom. Spoon all but one cup of rice into the mold and, using a large kitchen spoon, make a well in the center, pressing the rice against the bottom and sides of the mold. Fill with the liver in tomato sauce and cover with the remaining rice. Press the rice firmly and smooth it over to enclose the filling. Cover closely with foil and bake ten minutes.

9. Remove the mold and invert it onto a round hot plate (see note). Dribble a little of the hot sauce over the top of the mold and sprinkle with parsley. Serve remaining sauce on the side.

NOTE: Should the mold of rice break, smooth it over again into a mound shape.

This is a recipe of chef T. T. Wang of the Shun Lee Palace and Shun Lee Dynasty restaurants in New York.

Calf's Liver Hunan-Style

2 to 4 servings

¾ pound unsliced calf's liver
1 egg white
1 tablespoon cornstarch
2 tablespoons finely chopped chilies
2 tablespoons finely chopped green onions
½ teaspoon chopped fresh ginger
1 large clove garlic, finely chopped
1 teaspoon chili paste with garlic (see note)
1½ tablespoons shao hsing wine or dry sherry

1 tablespoon dark soy sauce
½ teaspoon sugar
½ teaspoon monosodium glutamate (optional)
1½ teaspoons cornstarch
2 teaspoons water
1 teaspoon sesame oil
⅛ teaspoon white pepper
½ teaspoon crushed Szechwan peppercorns (optional)
3½ cups peanut, vegetable, or corn oil
Sautéed spinach, Chinese-style (see following recipe)

1. Place the liver on a flat surface and cut into razor-thin slices, using a sharp knife. This is facilitated if the liver is partly frozen before slicing.

2. Put the liver slices in a mixing bowl and add the egg white and cornstarch. Blend well with the fingers.

3. Prepare the chilies, green onion, ginger, and garlic and set aside in a small dish.

4. Measure out the chili paste and set aside.

5. Blend the wine, soy sauce, sugar, and monosodium glutamate. Blend the cornstarch and water and add it. Add the sesame oil, white pepper, and Szechwan peppercorns and set aside.

6. Heat the oil in a very hot wok and swirl it around to coat the sides. When the oil is almost smoking, add the liver, stirring as rapidly as possible in a circular motion. Cook about fifteen seconds, no longer. Drain well, but leave about one tablespoon of oil in the wok.

7. Add the chilies, green onion, ginger, garlic, and chili paste and cook about five seconds. Add the soy-sauce mixture, stir to blend, and add the liver. Cook about five seconds or until liver is piping hot. Cook as briefly as possible.

8. Serve with spinach as a garnish.

NOTE: Chili paste with garlic is available in jars in Chinese grocery stores.

Sautéed Spinach Chinese-Style

2 to 4 servings

1 pound fresh spinach (do not attempt this recipe with frozen spinach)
3 tablespoons peanut, vegetable, or corn oil

1 tablespoon shao hsing wine or dry sherry
Salt to taste

1. Wash the spinach and drain well. It is best to pat the leaves with paper towels or use a salad spin-dryer. Set aside.

2. Heat the oil in a wok and, when it is very hot, swirl it around to coat the sides.

3. Add the spinach, stirring quickly. Cook about thirty seconds. Add the wine and salt. Toss and serve as soon as the leaves are wilted, about ten seconds longer.

This is the recipe of André Soltner, chef-proprietor of Lutèce restaurant in New York and a native of Alsace.

Quenelles de Foie de Veau à l'Alsacienne

(Calf's liver dumplings)

4 to 6 servings

½ pound calf's liver
3 cups thinly sliced onions
1 tablespoon peanut, vegetable, or corn oil
⅓ pound smoked bacon
1 clove garlic, split
1½ cups fine, fresh, soft bread crumbs
¼ cup milk
2 large, or 3 small, very cold eggs

⅛ teaspoon grated nutmeg
4 tablespoons flour
Salt and freshly ground pepper to taste
¼ cup finely chopped parsley
1 tablespoon butter
1 cup Demi-glace (page 197) or canned beef gravy

1. Cut away any veins and tough membranes from the liver. Cut the liver into cubes and set aside. The meat should be quite cold.

2. Cook two cups of the onions in a skillet with the oil. Cook, stirring often, until onions are wilted and golden brown. Let cool and chill.

3. To the container of a food processor, add the bacon, garlic, liver, and cooked onions. Purée until very fine in texture. Spoon and scrape the mixture into a mixing bowl.

4. Meanwhile, combine the bread crumbs and milk and blend thoroughly. Scrape this mixture into a clean cheesecloth and squeeze tightly to remove as much liquid as possible. Add the bread to the liver mixture and beat with a wire whisk to blend.

5. Add the eggs, nutmeg, flour, salt, and pepper. Add the parsley and beat well. The mixture will be quite liquid. Place it in the freezer until very cold, but do not freeze.

6. Bring two quarts of water, or enough to barely cover the dumplings, to the boil in a skillet. Add salt to taste.

7. Because of the liquid nature of the dumpling mixture, you must work very quickly. Using two soup spoons, dip one in the mixture and lift up a heaping spoonful. Using the second spoon, twirl it around inside the first to round out the mixture. Lower the second spoon into the simmering liquid and shake the dumpling free from the spoon. Rinse the second spoon in hot water after each use.

8. Simmer the dumplings gently for twelve minutes.

9. While the dumplings are cooking, melt the butter in a saucepan and add one cup of finely sliced onions. Cook briefly until onions are golden. Add the demi-glace and cook until thoroughly heated.

10. Serve the dumplings with the onion sauce and, if desired, sauerkraut.

KIDNEYS

It is altogether true, as a medical journal once said, that when it comes time to dine, both the soma and the psyche sit down at table. It has always seemed unfortunate, therefore, that one of the most eminently edible parts of the veal is labeled kidneys, a word that is a stumbling block where much of the public appetite is concerned. How much more elegant when something is known as *rognons de veau,* as veal kidneys are known in French.

Kidneys, like liver, generally demand high heat and fast cooking. The varieties of flavors that complement them are admirable. They can withstand the pungency of a mustard sauce, or be enhanced by the simple fragrance of juniper berries.

This recipe is from l'Oustau de Baumanière, in Les Baux, France.

Rognons de Veau à la Baumanière
(Veal kidneys with an herb, port, and cream sauce)

4 servings

2 kidneys, about 1¾ pounds total weight
Salt and freshly ground pepper to taste
¼ pound chicken livers
1 teaspoon olive oil
5 tablespoons butter
1 tablespoon finely chopped shallots
½ teaspoon chopped fresh tarragon or ¼ teaspoon dried
½ teaspoon chopped fresh basil or ¼ teaspoon dried
3 tablespoons Bourbon
½ cup dry white wine
1 tablespoon port
2 tablespoons Dijon or Düsseldorf mustard
½ cup heavy cream

1. Place the kidneys on a flat surface, core side up. With a sharp knife, cut away and discard part but not all of the white core. Sprinkle the kidneys with salt and pepper and set aside.

2. Cut the chicken livers into very thin slices. (This is facilitated if the livers are partly frozen.) Set aside.

3. Heat the oil and two tablespoons of the butter in a skillet and add the shallots. Cook briefly and add the tarragon and basil. Add the kid-

172

neys and cook, turning as necessary to brown evenly. Ten minutes is about the exact cooking time. The kidneys should remain rare in the center because they will be sliced later and reheated in sauce.

4. Remove the kidneys and cover with foil to keep warm.

5. To the skillet, add two tablespoons of Bourbon and ignite it. Cook until reduced by half. Add the white wine, port, and mustard and stir in the heavy cream. Cook briefly and swirl in two tablespoons of the butter.

6. Remove the sauce from the heat.

7. In another skillet, heat the remaining tablespoon of butter. Add the chicken livers and sprinkle with salt and pepper. Cook about forty-five seconds. Add one tablespoon of Bourbon and ignite it.

8. Pour the cream sauce over the chicken livers and cook briefly.

9. Place the kidneys on a slicing board. Discard the liquid that has accumulated around them. Cut the kidneys crosswise into quarter-inch slices. Transfer the kidneys to a small casserole.

10. Strain the sauce over the kidneys, using a spoon or rubber spatula to press the solids, including livers, to extract as much liquid as possible. It is best to use the strainer known in French kitchens as a chinois.

11. Reheat the kidneys briefly in the sauce.

12. Serve with Baked Rice (page 211).

Rognons de Veau à la Moutarde

(Veal kidneys in mustard sauce)

4 servings

2 veal kidneys, about
  1½ pounds
2 tablespoons peanut, vegetable,
  or corn oil
3 tablespoons butter
¼ pound mushrooms, thinly
  sliced
2 tablespoons finely chopped
  shallots

1 tablespoon Cognac
1 cup heavy cream
1 tablespoon imported prepared
  mustard, such as Dijon or
  Düsseldorf
Toast

1. Split the kidneys in half lengthwise. Cut away most of the tough white center core but leave a thin layer intact. Cut the kidney halves into cubes, one inch or slightly smaller.

2. Heat the oil until hot and almost smoking in a heavy skillet. Add the kidneys and cook, stirring often, about three minutes. Cook only to

the rare stage—remember, they will be cooked once more. If overcooked at any point they will become dry. Pour the kidneys into a sieve and set aside to drain.

3. Add two tablespoons of butter to another heavy skillet and add the mushrooms. Cook, stirring, about two minutes and add the shallots. Cook three minutes, stirring often, and sprinkle with Cognac. Add the cream and cook, stirring, about three minutes.

4. Add the kidneys, bring to the boil, and add the mustard, stirring to blend. Swirl in the remaining butter and serve hot on toast.

Rognons de Veau
à la Diable

(Grilled deviled veal kidneys)

4 servings

4 veal kidneys, about 2 pounds total weight
4 teaspoons imported prepared mustard, such as Dijon or Düsseldorf
1½ cups fine fresh bread crumbs
4 tablespoons peanut, vegetable, or corn oil
Watercress for garnish
Grilled tomatoes for garnish
8 slices freshly cooked crisp bacon

1. Place the kidneys on a flat surface and, using a sharp knife, butterfly them. That is to say, slice them almost but not quite in half and open them up. Spread each kidney with one teaspoon of mustard. Dredge the kidneys all over in bread crumbs.

2. Dribble one tablespoon of oil over both sides of the kidneys. Run two skewers through the kidneys in the shape of a cross to help keep them from curling as they cook.

3. Preheat the broiler to high or preheat a charcoal grill. Broil or grill the kidneys close to the coals until cooked to the desired degree of doneness, turning them as necessary. Serve garnished with watercress and grilled tomatoes. Arrange two slices of bacon on top of each kidney. Serve with mustard on the side.

Rognons de Veau Maison Bergerac

(Veal kidneys with a mustard and wine sauce)

4 to 6 servings

2 well-trimmed kidneys, about 1¼ pounds
Salt and freshly ground pepper to taste
1 tablespoon butter
½ pound mushrooms, thinly sliced, about 4 cups
2 tablespoons finely chopped shallots
2 tablespoons peanut, vegetable, or corn oil
½ teaspoon thyme

1 tablespoon Cognac
3 tablespoons finely chopped parsley
Juice of half a lemon
½ bay leaf
¼ cup dry white wine
2 tablespoons Madeira
1 tablespoon imported prepared mustard, such as Dijon or Düsseldorf
¼ cup heavy cream

1. Preheat the oven to 350 degrees.

2. Slice the kidneys in half. Carefully trim away most of the white core and any membrane. Cut each half into thin slices and sprinkle with salt and pepper.

3. Heat the butter and add the mushrooms. Cook about five minutes until dry and golden. Add the shallots and cook briefly.

4. Heat the oil in another skillet and, when it is quite hot, add the kidneys. Cook over high heat, stirring often, about three minutes. Pour into a sieve and drain thoroughly.

5. Combine the mushrooms and kidneys in a flameproof and heat-proof casserole. Add the thyme and Cognac, parsley, lemon juice, bay leaf, and wine. Bring to the boil on top of the stove. Blend the Madeira, mustard, and cream and stir it in. Cover closely and bake in the oven for twenty-five to thirty minutes.

6. Serve with Buttered Fine Noodles (page 209).

This recipe is from Comme Chez Soi in Brussels, Belgium.

Rognons de Veau aux Baies de Genevrier

(Veal kidneys with juniper berries)

6 servings

3 veal kidneys, about 2 pounds
Salt and freshly ground pepper
   to taste
4 tablespoons butter
½ pound mushrooms, sliced or
   quartered, about 3 cups

18 juniper berries
⅓ cup Madeira
¾ cup Demi-glace (page 197) or
   canned beef gravy

1. Place the kidneys on a flat surface and carefully cut away and discard part, but not all, of the white core that runs down the center. Cut the kidneys crosswise into three-quarter-inch lengths. Sprinkle with salt and pepper.

2. Select a large, heavy skillet. Add half the butter and, when it is very hot, add the kidney pieces. Cook over high heat, turning the pieces as they brown. Brown well, about five minutes, but do not overcook. The pieces must remain a bit rare or they will be dry.

3. Meanwhile, heat the remaining butter in another skillet and add the mushrooms. Cook about three minutes, stirring often.

4. Using a two-pronged fork, remove the kidney pieces and set aside. They will give up a good deal of liquid, which should be discarded.

5. Add the mushrooms to the skillet in which the kidneys cooked. Add the juniper berries and stir over high heat. Add the Madeira and demi-glace. Cook down over high heat by about half. Add salt and pepper to taste. Add the drained kidneys. Cook until piping hot.

6. Serve with Baked Rice (page 211).

Rognons de Veau Ardennaise

(*Roast kidneys with ham*)

4 servings

4 veal kidneys, about 3 pounds
    total weight
5 tablespoons butter
4 to 6 thin slices prosciutto or
    other ham
8 crushed juniper berries
1 tablespoon finely chopped
    shallots

3 tablespoons Cognac
½ cup Veal Broth (page 197) or
    chicken broth
2 tablespoons finely chopped
    parsley

1. Preheat the oven to 450 degrees.

2. Trim the kidneys of most of their white inner core but leave a thin layer.

3. Heat one tablespoon of butter in a large skillet and add the kidneys. Cook about ten minutes, or until nicely golden all over. Place in the oven and bake fifteen minutes. Take care not to overcook the kidneys. They should be slightly pink inside when ready. Pour off the fat. Remove the kidneys and set the skillet aside.

4. Heat one tablespoon of butter in a baking dish large enough to hold the kidneys. Arrange the ham slices over the butter to cover the bottom and to warm the ham slightly. The slices should be slightly overlapping. Arrange the kidneys over the ham.

5. To the skillet in which the kidneys cooked, add one tablespoon of the butter, the juniper berries, the shallots, and two tablespoons of the Cognac. Add the broth. Simmer to reduce by about half. Swirl the remaining butter into the sauce.

6. Sprinkle the remaining tablespoon of Cognac over the kidneys and pour the sauce over. Serve sprinkled with parsley.

7. Serve with rice.

This recipe, from the town of Bauge, in France, was a great specialty of Le Pavillon restaurant in New York during the days when it was generally conceded to be the finest French restaurant in America.

Rognons Bauge

(Roast kidneys in a mustard-cream sauce)

6 servings

3 veal kidneys, trimmed of all
fat
Salt and freshly ground pepper
to taste
2 tablespoons peanut, vegetable,
or corn oil
1 tablespoon butter
2 tablespoons chopped shallots

2 tablespoons Cognac
2 tablespoons Demi-glace (page
197) or canned beef gravy
1 cup heavy cream
1 tablespoon imported prepared
mustard, such as Dijon or
Düsseldorf

1. Sprinkle the kidneys with salt and pepper.

2. Heat the oil in a heavy skillet large enough to hold the kidneys in one layer. Add the kidneys and brown quickly but well all over.

3. Cook for ten minutes, turning frequently. Remove the kidneys and keep warm. Pour off the oil and other liquid that may have accumulated in the pan.

4. Add the butter and shallots. Cook briefly and sprinkle with Cognac. Add the demi-glace and simmer one minute. Add the cream and cook over high heat about five minutes. Add salt and pepper to taste. Stir in the mustard and remove from the heat. Do not cook further.

5. Quickly slice the kidneys crosswise, cutting them into one-half-inch pieces. Spoon the sauce over and serve.

6. An excellent accompaniment to this dish is Braised Fennel (page 216).

TONGUE

Calf's tongue has a very special appeal because of its texture and delicate flavor. Like many other parts of the veal, it is complemented by the sharpness of a vinaigrette sauce or, when breaded and baked, with a mustard sauce. Braised tongue with carrots can be an elegant feast for any season.

Langues de Veau Braisées aux Carottes

(Braised calf's tongue with carrots)

4 to 6 servings

2 calf's tongues, about 1¼ pounds each
6 thin slices salt pork, about 2 ounces
Salt and freshly ground pepper to taste
1 cup coarsely chopped onion
½ cup carrot cut into rounds
¼ cup coarsely chopped celery
1 clove garlic, peeled
½ cup plus 2 tablespoons dry white wine

2 cups Demi-glace (page 197) or canned beef gravy
1 cup water
⅓ cup tomato purée
2 sprigs fresh thyme or ½ teaspoon dried
1 bay leaf
4 sprigs fresh parsley
2 pounds carrots, trimmed, scraped, quartered, and cut in half, about 4 cups
2 teaspoons cornstarch

1. Preheat the oven to 400 degrees.

2. Place the tongues in a kettle and add cold water to cover. Bring to the boil and simmer about five minutes. Drain and set aside.

3. Put the slices of salt pork in a heavy casserole large enough to hold the tongues. Cook until rendered of fat. Add the tongues and sprinkle with salt and pepper. Brown all over, about ten minutes.

4. Add the onion, carrot, celery, and garlic. Cook, stirring occasionally, until the vegetables are browned, about ten minutes. Pour off the fat from the casserole.

5. Add the one-half cup wine, demi-glace, water, tomato purée, thyme, bay leaf, and parsley. Bring to the boil and cover. Place in the oven and bake one hour and forty-five minutes, or until tongues are quite tender.

6. Remove the tongues and let cool.

7. Strain the sauce (there should be about two cups). Skim off the fat.

8. Peel the tongues and discard the peelings.

9. Place the carrot pieces in a saucepan and add water to cover. Bring to the boil and simmer about two minutes. Drain.

10. Place the tongues and carrots in a small casserole and add the two cups of strained sauce. Bring to the boil on top of the stove. Blend the cornstarch and two tablespoons wine and stir it into the sauce. Place the casserole in the oven and cook, uncovered, ten to fifteen minutes, basting occasionally.

11. Slice the tongues and serve with carrots and sauce.

12. Serve with boiled potatoes.

Langue de Veau Pochée

(*Poached calf's tongue*)

4 appetizer servings

1 calf's tongue, about 1¼ pounds	4 sprigs fresh parsley
4 cups water, or enough to cover	1 whole clove
¼ cup coarsely chopped celery	Salt to taste
½ cup coarsely chopped onion	12 crushed peppercorns
½ cup carrot cut into rounds	1 clove garlic, peeled
1 bay leaf	Sauce Vinaigrette (page 198)
2 sprigs fresh thyme or ½ teaspoon dried	1 tablespoon finely chopped parsley
	1 hard-cooked egg, chopped

1. Place the tongue in a kettle and add cold water to cover. Bring to the boil and simmer about five minutes. Drain.

2. Return the tongue to a clean kettle and add the four cups water, celery, onion, carrot, bay leaf, thyme, parsley sprigs, clove, salt, peppercorns, and garlic. Bring to the boil and simmer until quite tender throughout, about one and one-half hours.

3. Let the tongue cool in its liquid to lukewarm. Serve lukewarm or cold. To serve, cut the tongue into quarter-inch slices and serve with the vinaigrette sauce spooned over. Garnish with chopped parsley and chopped egg.

Langues de Veau à la Diable

(Calf's Tongues with mustard sauce)

4 to 6 servings

2 calf's tongues, about 1¼ pounds each
6 thin slices salt pork, about 2 ounces
Salt and freshly ground pepper to taste
1 cup coarsely chopped onion
½ cup carrot cut into rounds
¼ cup coarsely chopped celery
1 clove garlic, peeled
½ cup dry white wine
2 cups Demi-glace (page 197) or canned beef gravy

1 cup water
⅓ cup tomato purée
2 sprigs fresh thyme or ½ teaspoon dried
1 bay leaf
4 sprigs fresh parsley
2 tablespoons imported prepared mustard, such as Dijon or Düsseldorf
4 tablespoons fine fresh bread crumbs
¼ cup butter, melted
Sauce Diable I (page 201)

1. Preheat the oven to 400 degrees.

2. Place the tongues in a kettle and add cold water to cover. Bring to the boil and simmer about five minutes. Drain and set aside.

3. Add the salt pork to a heavy casserole large enough to hold the tongues. Cook until rendered of fat. Add the tongues and sprinkle with salt and pepper. Brown all over, about ten minutes.

4. Add the onion, carrot, celery, and garlic. Cook, stirring occasionally, until the vegetables are browned, about ten minutes. Pour off the fat from the casserole.

5. Add the wine, demi-glace, water, tomato purée, thyme, bay leaf, and parsley. Bring to the boil and cover. Place in the oven and bake one hour and forty-five minutes, or until tongues are quite tender.

6. Remove the tongues and let cool.

7. Strain the sauce and reserve one cup for the sauce diable. Skim off the fat.

8. Peel the tongues and discard the peelings. Slice the tongues down the center. Open them up and run a skewer through each tongue to keep it flat while broiling.

9. Preheat the broiler.

10. Brush the tongues all over with the mustard. Coat them on all sides with the bread crumbs. Dribble the melted butter evenly over both sides of the tongues. Broil the tongues until nicely browned and crisp on both sides.

11. Slice and serve hot with sauce diable.

CALF'S FEET, HEAD, AND HEART

There is no bistro in France that does not have *pieds de veau*, known in English as calf's feet, on its menu. They are as much a part of the workingman's or country-style kitchen as fried chicken in the American South or the seven sweets and sours of the Pennsylvania Dutch dinner table.

Basic though they may be, they can be turned into the most elegant fare, such as calf's feet in a poulette sauce—a satiny-smooth creation made with cream and eggs.

Curiously, although tripe is a product of beef, the calf's foot is essential to many tripe dishes. Its gelatin and meat give body to *tripes à la mode de Caen*, which to many palates is more to be treasured than the truffles of Périgord or the foie gras of Strasbourg. Similarly, calf's feet are essential to one of the great regional specialities of America: the celebrated Philadelphia pepper pot, made with tripe, calf's feet, and dried hot red pepper.

To many minds, there is nothing in classic French cooking to whet the appetite like *tête de veau vinaigrette*. This, of course, is the boned head of a calf, including the tongue and brain, served with a vinaigrette sauce or that marvel among mayonnaise preparations, a sauce gribiche.

Calves' hearts may not be for all tastes, but we include them here in a Viennese version of braised hearts.

Pieds de Veau Poulette

(Calf's feet in cream and egg sauce)

8 or more servings

4 calf's feet, about 1¾ pounds
  each
⅓ cup plus 2 tablespoons flour
3 quarts water
1 onion, stuck with 2 cloves
1 large carrot, trimmed, scraped,
  and quartered
2 cloves garlic, split
1 bay leaf
3 sprigs fresh thyme or ½ teaspoon dried

10 peppercorns
Salt to taste
4 sprigs parsley
1 tablespoon butter
3 egg yolks
3 tablespoons lemon juice plus
  the juice of 1 whole lemon
Freshly ground pepper to taste
1 cup heavy cream
⅛ teaspoon grated nutmeg
¼ cup finely chopped parsley

1. A calf's foot when purchased generally includes the hoofs and a thin upper leg bone enclosed with flesh and skin. When ready to make this dish, the hoofs should be split in two. Using a sharp boning knife, carve away the meat and skin from the upper leg bones of each calf's foot. Save all the pieces, including the leg bones.

2. Place the pieces in a deep kettle and add cold water to cover. Bring to the boil and simmer five minutes. Drain.

3. Return the pieces to a clean kettle.

4. Spoon one-third cup of the flour into a sieve and place the sieve over the kettle. Gradually add the water to the sieve, stirring to dissolve the flour into the kettle. This will prevent lumping. Add the onion, carrot, garlic, bay leaf, thyme, peppercorns, salt, and parsley. Bring to the boil and simmer one and one-half hours, skimming the surface as necessary to remove scum and foam.

5. Drain and reserve the broth. Discard the leg bones. When cool enough to handle, remove and reserve all the gelatin-like skin and meat from the hoofs. Cut the gelatin-like skin and meat into two-inch cubes. Discard all bones.

6. Cook the broth over high heat about ten minutes. Reserve two cups for the sauce. Discard the remaining broth or reserve it for use in soups or sauces.

7. Melt the butter in a saucepan and add the remaining two tablespoons of flour, stirring with a wire whisk. Add the reserved two cups of broth, stirring rapidly with the whisk. When thickened and smooth, let simmer about five minutes.

8. Beat the egg yolks with three tablespoons of lemon juice. Add salt, pepper to taste, cream, and nutmeg. Gradually beat in about a cup of the hot sauce.

9. Add the egg and sauce mixture to the sauce remaining in the saucepan, stirring vigorously. Cook over very low heat, stirring with a wooden spoon, until the mixture coats the spoon like a custard. Do not overcook or the sauce may curdle.

10. Add the cubed meat to the sauce and bring to the boil. Add the juice of one lemon and sprinkle with parsley.

11. Serve with Baked Rice (page 211).

This curiously compelling dish is of Lithuanian Jewish origin. It is basically calf's-foot jelly to be served as an appetizer, nicely spiced with garlic and garnished with sliced egg and onions. It is best served with grated horseradish. Petcha (the accent is on the last syllable) is sometimes referred to as fissnugge and sülze. In some homes it is served hot, unjelled, like a soup. But cold is better. This version is a family recipe of Eleanor Lynn Helprin, the actress.

Petcha

18 or more servings

2 calf's feet, about 4½ pounds total weight	10 large cloves garlic, finely chopped
14 cups water	3 tablespoons vinegar
Salt and freshly ground pepper to taste	Juice of 2 lemons
2 onions, peeled, about ¼ pound	3 hard-cooked eggs, sliced
	1 small onion, sliced
1 or 2 bay leaves	2 teaspoons paprika
	Horseradish for garnish

1. Have each calf's foot cut crosswise into thirds. Place the feet in a basin and add cold water to cover. Let stand two hours and drain.

2. Put the feet in a small kettle or large saucepan and add the water. Add salt and pepper, onions, bay leaves, garlic, vinegar, and lemon juice. The flavor of garlic is essential to this dish.

3. Bring to the boil and simmer four hours, skimming the surface as necessary. Strain and reserve both the feet and the cooking liquid. Let cool.

4. Remove the meat and gelatin from the bones. Discard the bones. Cut or pull the meat and gelatin into small pieces. Discard any hard or very firm portions of meat, gristle, or tendons.

5. Blend the reserved meat and cooking liquid.

6. Pour the mixture into a rectangular dish measuring about 14 x 8 x 1½ inches. Carefully float the egg and onion slices over the top. Sprinkle with paprika and chill until quite cold and firm.

7. Serve sliced into cubes or rectangles with buttered toast. Serve with horseradish and, if desired, additional salt sprinkled over.

It is curious that one of the great regional specialties of America should be made with tripe, for Americans in the early days were not much given to adventurous eating. The pepper in the name comes from the dried hot red pepper used to season the dish.

Philadelphia Pepper Pot

6 to 8 servings

4 tablespoons butter
1 cup finely chopped onion
1 onion, stuck with 2 cloves
½ cup finely chopped celery
½ cup finely chopped carrot
½ cup chopped sweet green or red pepper
3½ tablespoons flour
5 cups Veal Broth (page 197) or chicken broth.
1 calf's foot cut into 3 pieces, about 2 pounds
¾ pound honeycomb tripe, cut into bite-size cubes

1 whole clove garlic, peeled
1 dried hot red pepper or more to taste
1 bay leaf
1 teaspoon dried marjoram
1 teaspoon dried basil
½ teaspoon dried thyme
Salt and freshly ground pepper to taste
2 cups peeled potatoes, cut into ½-inch cubes
1 cup heavy cream

1. Heat the butter in a deep kettle or casserole and, when it is hot but not brown, add the chopped onion, whole onion with cloves, celery, carrot, and green or red pepper. Cook, stirring, about ten minutes. Do not brown.

2. Sprinkle with flour and stir to coat the vegetables evenly. Add the veal broth, stirring constantly to prevent lumping. Add the calf's foot, tripe, garlic, hot red pepper, bay leaf, marjoram, basil, thyme, salt, and pepper. Bring to the boil and simmer, covered, two to four hours, or until tripe is tender.

3. Remove the whole onion with cloves and the bay leaf. Remove the calf's foot; pull off the meat and gelatin-like skin, shred them, and return them to the pot.

4. Add the potatoes and cook until tender. Add the heavy cream and bring to the boil. Serve piping hot in hot soup bowls with crusty French bread. More ground pepper may be added before serving.

This is one of the great regional specialties of French cooking—tripe robustly seasoned and flavored in the end with Calvados or applejack. It is a specialty, of course, of the town of Caen, which is the capital of Calvados, the region of the greatest applejack in the world.

Tripes à la Mode de Caen

(Baked tripe flavored with Calvados)

8 to 10 servings

10 pounds honeycomb tripe
3 calf's feet, about 1¾ pounds each
1½ pounds leeks
3 sprigs fresh thyme or 1 teaspoon dried
2 bay leaves
1 pound onions, peeled
2 cloves

¾ pound carrots, trimmed, scraped, and cut in half
10 sprigs parsley
1 bottle dry white wine
Salt and freshly ground pepper to taste
3 quarts water
1½ cups Calvados or applejack

1. Cut away and discard most of the fat that may remain on the tripe. Cut the tripe into two-inch cubes. Set aside.

2. A calf's foot when purchased generally encompasses the hoofs and a thin upper leg bone enclosed with flesh and skin. When ready to make this dish, the hoofs should be split in two. Using a sharp boning knife, carve away the meat and skin from the upper leg bones of each calf's foot. Save all the pieces, including the leg bones.

3. Place the calf's feet and leg bones and reserved meat in a large kettle and add the cubed tripe. Add water to cover and bring to the boil. Simmer five minutes and drain.

4. Line a large colander with a square of cheesecloth for the vegetables and seasonings.

5. Trim the leeks and cut off the green part of the leaves. Wash the green part well and cut the leaves into one-and-one-half-inch lengths. Put them in the colander. Reserve the white part for another use, such as in soups.

6. Add the thyme and bay leaves.

7. Stick one of the onions with the cloves and add it along with the remaining onions to the cheesecloth. Add the carrots and parsley. Bring up the edges of the cheesecloth and tie at the top to make a bag.

8. Select a large kettle with a tight-fitting lid and place the meat, calf's feet, and leg bones on the bottom. Scatter the tripe over and around this. Add the cheesecloth bag. Add the wine, salt, pepper, water, and one-half cup of Calvados. The solid ingredients should be barely covered with liquid.

9. Meanwhile, preheat the oven to 350 degrees.

10. Bring the liquid to the boil on top of the stove and cover closely. Bake nine hours, or until the tripe is almost fork-tender. Remove and discard the cheesecloth bag.

11. Let cool and remove the calf's feet. Pick off and reserve all the gelatin-like skin and meat from the feet. Discard all the bones. Cut the gelatin-like skin and meat into two-inch cubes. Return this to the kettle and continue cooking on top of the stove about one hour, skimming the surface to remove all trace of fat and scum. Add the remaining cup of Calvados and stir.

12. Serve with plain boiled potatoes and imported prepared mustard, such as Dijon or Düsseldorf.

Tête de Veau Vinaigrette

(Poached calf's head with
sauce vinaigrette)

12 or more servings

1 set calf's brains
1 6½-pound boned calf's head, including the tongue
½ cup flour
1 onion, stuck with 4 cloves
1 carrot, trimmed and scraped
2 sprigs fresh thyme or 1 teaspoon dried
1 bay leaf
12 crushed peppercorns
Salt to taste
Sauce Vinaigrette (page 198) and/or Sauce Gribiche (page 200)

1. Prepare the brains (see page 149), but do not cook them until just before serving with the calf's head.

2. The calf's head may be left whole or, if the cooking kettle is small, cut in half. Add the head to the kettle and add cold water to cover it well. Bring to the boil and simmer five minutes. Remove from the heat and let cool. The head in its liquid may be chilled overnight.

3. Remove the head and open it up to expose the interior. Cut and scrape away the tough white papillae, or bristle-like coating, on the inside of the mouth.

4. Carve the cut head into rather large serving pieces as follows: Leave the tongue intact. Cut off and reserve the snout. Cut the head in half if this has not already been done; cut each half into three or four lengthwise pieces; cut these pieces into serving pieces, measuring roughly one and one-half by four inches.

5. Put the tongue, the snout, and the cut-up head into a kettle. Place the flour in a sieve and hold it over the kettle. Pour twenty cups of water over the flour, letting it flow through. This will prevent the flour from lumping. The flour is used to keep the pieces of head white. Add the onion stuck with cloves, carrot, thyme, bay leaf, peppercorns, and salt. Bring to the boil and cook one hour. Cover and cook one hour longer, or until the meat and skin of the head are fork-tender. Set aside.

6. Cook the brain. Serve slices of brain and tongue alongside the other pieces of head. Serve with boiled potatoes and sauce vinaigrette and/or sauce gribiche.

This is a recipe of Arno Schmidt, executive chef of the Waldorf-Astoria in New York.

Viennese Braised Veal Hearts

6 or more servings

2 veal hearts, about 3 pounds
Salt and freshly ground pepper
  to taste
4 strips bacon, cut into slivers
3 tablespoons finely chopped
  onion
1 teaspoon chopped garlic
3 tablespoons Hungarian paprika

1 tablespoon flour
1 tablespoon tomato paste
½ teaspoon caraway seeds
½ teaspoon dried marjoram
2 cups sauerkraut, about ¾
  pound
1 cup dry white wine
1 cup sour cream

1. If the large artery protrudes from the hearts, cut it off flush with the base of the heart. Sprinkle the hearts with salt and pepper.

2. Cook the bacon in a casserole or Dutch oven large enough to hold the hearts in one layer. When the bacon is golden, add the hearts and cook to brown all over, about twelve minutes.

3. Remove the hearts and sprinkle the bottom of the casserole with onion and garlic. Cook until golden. Add the paprika and flour, stirring.

4. Add the tomato paste, caraway seeds, and marjoram. Scatter the sauerkraut over the bottom and add the hearts. Pour wine over all. Cover closely and cook over low heat, about one and one-half hours, or until hearts are tender.

5. Remove the hearts and stir the sour cream into the sauerkraut. Serve the hearts sliced with the sauce.

6. Serve with boiled potatoes.

•Soups•

Because of the nature of veal and veal bones, almost any soup would benefit by the addition of the bones along with the other ingredients. Veal bones yield a natural gelatin that gives both body and "strength" to the soup.

Although many people may believe that mock turtle soup is something coined by Lewis Carroll for *Alice's Adventures in Wonderland,* he actually used the character Mock Turtle because of the soup, which had widespread currency in English kitchens before Alice came about. Mock turtle soup is a delectable creation. It is made with a calf's head, the meat of which has much the texture of the turtle found in green-turtle soup. The ingredients include the classic spices that are thought of as the characteristic flavors of real turtle soup.

Once mock turtle is made, it can be turned into an irresistible soup of another sort, Lady Curzon's soup. This is a curried soup enriched with cream and eggs. Lady Curzon, by the way, was a Chicagoan born in 1870 whose original name was Mary Leiter. She was the wife of Lord Curzon, the British viceroy to India. As such, she occupied the most powerful position ever held by any American woman in the British Empire.

Less august, perhaps, but also delicious, are two more veal soups in this chapter: the traditional *zuppa di fagioli e riso,* made with meaty veal bones, beans, and rice, and another with veal dumplings and escarole.

Mock Turtle Soup

8 or more servings

½ calf's head, boned, about ¾
  pound (see note)
1 calf's tongue, cleaned
3 quarts Veal Broth (page 197) or
  chicken broth
Salt and freshly ground pepper
  to taste
2 tablespoons butter
3 tablespoons finely chopped
  shallots
1 cup finely chopped onion
¼ pound cooked ham, diced,
  about 1 cup
1 cup thinly sliced mushrooms
1 tablespoon dried sage
3 whole allspice

3 whole cloves
1 teaspoon dried marjoram
1 teaspoon chopped fresh thyme
  or ½ teaspoon dried
1 teaspoon dried summer savory
  (optional)
1 bay leaf
¼ cup chopped fresh parsley
2 teaspoons chopped fresh basil
  or 1 teaspoon dried
⅛ teaspoon cayenne
2 tablespoons flour
¼ teaspoon ground mace
1 cup Madeira, plus additional
  wine to serve on the side

1. Place the boned calf's head and calf's tongue in a kettle and add cold water to cover. Bring to the boil and simmer five minutes. Drain well and run under cold running water until thoroughly chilled. Drain well.

2. Cut the meat from the head into one-inch cubes, discarding any fatty portions. Cut away and discard the white bristly portion around the mouth.

3. Return the cubed meat and the whole tongue to a clean kettle.

4. Add the broth, salt, and pepper and bring to the boil. Simmer one and one-half hours, covered.

5. Meanwhile, melt the butter in a saucepan and add the shallots and onion. Cook until wilted and add the ham and mushrooms. Tie the sage, allspice, and cloves together in a small cheesecloth bag. Add it. Add the marjoram, thyme, savory, bay leaf, parsley, basil, and cayenne. Cook ten minutes, stirring often.

6. Sprinkle the mixture with the flour, stirring. Spoon off two cups of the broth from the calf's head and add it to the mixture, stirring. Cover and cook one hour. Remove the cheesecloth bag and bay leaf.

7. Pour the mixture into the container of a food processor and blend thoroughly. Add this to the soup.

8. Add the mace, one cup of Madeira, and salt and pepper to taste.

9. Remove the tongue from the soup and cut it in half. Use one half for other purposes, such as sandwiches. Cut one half into cubes and return it to the soup.

10. Serve the piping-hot soup in bowls with more Madeira on the side. This soup keeps well when refrigerated. It can also be used to prepare Lady Curzon's Soup (see following recipe).

NOTE: The bones from the calf's head may be used to prepare the veal broth.

Lady Curzon's Soup

4 to 6 servings

1 tablespoon butter	½ cup heavy cream
½ cup finely diced mushrooms	1 egg yolk
2 tablespoons curry powder	1 cup whipped cream (optional)
3 cups Mock Turtle Soup with meat (see preceding recipe) or canned turtle soup	

1. Heat the butter in a saucepan and add the mushrooms. Cook until wilted.

2. Sprinkle with curry powder. Cook briefly, stirring with a wire whisk. Add the soup, stirring constantly with the whisk.

3. Blend the half cup of cream with the egg yolk. Remove the soup from the heat and add the yolk mixture, stirring constantly. Return the soup to the heat and cook briefly until piping hot but not quite boiling. If the soup boils, the yolk may curdle.

4. Pour the soup into cups (this soup is traditionally served in demitasse cups) and serve. Or, and this is also traditional, float equal amounts of whipped cream on top of each serving and run briefly under a hot broiler until the cream starts to brown.

Zuppa di Fagioli e Riso

(Rice and bean soup)

6 to 8 servings

1 cup dried white pea beans
8 cups cold water
2 pounds meaty veal bones
1 large carrot, trimmed, scraped, and quartered
1 rib celery
1 onion, stuck with 3 cloves
2 sprigs parsley
10 peppercorns, tied in cheese-cloth
Salt to taste
1 whole garlic clove

2 cups tomatoes
¼ teaspoon red pepper flakes or more to taste
3 tablespoons butter
1 cup finely chopped onion
1 cup finely chopped celery with leaves
2 teaspoons minced garlic
Freshly ground pepper to taste
½ cup raw rice
¼ cup finely chopped parsley
Freshly grated Parmesan cheese

1. Place the beans in a mixing bowl and add cold water to cover to a depth of one inch above the top of the beans. Let stand overnight.

2. Drain the beans and put them in a large saucepan or small kettle. Add eight cups of cold water and the veal bones, quartered carrot, rib of celery, onion stuck with cloves, parsley sprigs, peppercorns, salt, and garlic. Cook uncovered, skimming the surface as necessary, about one and one-half hours. Remove and discard the bones, carrot, celery, onion, parsley, and peppercorns.

3. Add the tomatoes and pepper flakes and bring to the boil.

4. Heat the butter in a small skillet and add the chopped onion, chopped celery, and minced garlic. Cook until onion is translucent and add it to the soup. Add salt and pepper to taste. Add the rice and cook until the rice is done, about twenty minutes. Sprinkle with chopped parsley. Serve hot with grated Parmesan cheese on the side.

Veal Dumplings and Escarole Soup

8 servings

1 pound lean veal
2 eggs
1 tablespoon coarsely chopped
   shallots
Salt and freshly ground pepper
   to taste
⅛ teaspoon nutmeg

2 cups fine fresh bread crumbs
Freshly grated Parmesan cheese
1 tablespoon chopped parsley
¾-pound head escarole
8 cups Veal Broth (page 197) or
   chicken broth

1. Cut the veal into cubes and put it in a food processor or electric blender. Add the eggs, shallots, salt, pepper, nutmeg, bread crumbs, one tablespoon Parmesan cheese, and parsley. Blend, stirring down as necessary.

2. Cut away the core from the escarole. Remove any tough ends and blemished leaves. Coarsely shred the escarole. There should be about eight cups.

3. Bring the veal broth to the boil and add the escarole. Simmer about ten minutes.

4. Meanwhile, prepare the veal mixture. Using the hands or two spoons, fashion the mixture into miniature football shapes, or pointed ovals. Use about one and one-half teaspoons of the mixture for each dumpling. Dipping the fingers or spoons into a basin of cold water will facilitate shaping. There should be forty to sixty dumplings.

5. Add the dumplings to the soup and continue to cook ten to fifteen minutes longer. Serve the soup in hot plates with grated Parmesan on the side.

•Sauces•

There are numerous sauces that are inevitably suited to veal cookery. Some are to be served over the veal, others to be used as a basis for one veal dish or another.

There are two fundamental sauce bases that occur with great frequency in veal cookery. One is a concentrated consommé, or broth, made with veal bones. The other is a dark concentrate, also made with veal bones and seasonings. Despite the time required for their preparation, they are quite easily made. They keep for many days in the refrigerator and, when frozen, for an indefinite period. They are not totally essential to the preparation of any dishes in this book. Fresh or canned chicken broth could be substituted for the veal broth as indicated, and canned beef gravy for the demi-glace. But they do add a purity that is desirable.

The other sauces in this chapter range from a basic mornay to the hot butter sauces, hollandaise and béarnaise, to a variety of tomato sauces.

Veal Broth

6 cups

3 pounds veal bones
16 cups water
1 cup coarsely chopped celery
1 cup coarsely chopped onion
1 cup coarsely chopped carrot
1 bay leaf
1 clove garlic, peeled and
    crushed
4 sprigs thyme or ½ teaspoon
    dried
6 sprigs parsley

1. Put the bones in a kettle and add cold water to cover. Bring to the boil and simmer about two minutes. Drain. Run the bones under cold water to chill. Drain.

2. Return the bones to a clean kettle and add the sixteen cups of water and the remaining ingredients. Bring to the boil and simmer three hours or longer. When ready, the liquid should be reduced to six cups. Strain. The broth may be frozen.

Demi-glace

5 cups

10 pounds meaty veal bones,
    chopped into 3- or 4-inch
    pieces
2 cups coarsely chopped carrots
4 cups coarsely chopped onion
2 cups coarsely chopped celery
10 peppercorns
2 bay leaves
2 cloves garlic, unpeeled, cut in
    half
4 sprigs fresh thyme or 1 tea-
    spoon dried
32 cups water
1 cup loosely packed parsley
    leaves
4 cups coarsely chopped toma-
    toes

1. Preheat the oven to 400 degrees.

2. Put the bones in a large, flat roasting pan. Place in the oven and bake two and one-half hours. Stir and turn bones every thirty minutes.

3. Scatter the carrots, onions, celery, peppercorns, bay leaves, garlic, and thyme over all. Bake thirty minutes longer.

4. Transfer the contents of the roasting pan to a large kettle. Add two cups of the water to the roasting pan and stir to dissolve the brown particles that cling to the bottom and sides of the pan. Add this to the kettle.

5. Add the remaining thirty cups of water. Add the parsley and tomatoes. Do not add salt. Bring to the boil and simmer over low heat for

twelve to sixteen hours, depending on intensity of heat. It is best if this simmers very slowly on a heating pad. That would take the maximum cooking time. Skim the surface often for the first two or three hours. Then it may simmer very slowly overnight.

6. Strain the liquid into jars. This stock will keep for weeks in the refrigerator and will keep indefinitely in the freezer.

Velouté de Veau
(*Veal sauce*)

3 cups

6 tablespoons butter	4 cups Veal Broth (page 197) or
8 tablespoons flour	chicken broth

1. Melt the butter in a saucepan and add the flour, stirring with a wire whisk.

2. When blended, add the broth, stirring rapidly with the whisk. When thickened and smooth, continue cooking thirty minutes, stirring often around the bottom to prevent sticking.

Sauce Vinaigrette

About 1 cup

3 tablespoons red wine vinegar	1 tablespoon chopped parsley
Salt and freshly ground pepper	1 teaspoon chopped chives
to taste	1 teaspoon chopped fresh tar-
¾ cup olive oil	ragon or ½ teaspoon dried

Pour the vinegar into a mixing bowl and add salt and pepper. Gradually add the oil, stirring rapidly. Add the herbs and serve at room temperature.

Béarnaise Sauce

About ¾ cup

½ pound butter	3 teaspoons chopped fresh tar-
2 tablespoons red wine vinegar	ragon or 1½ teaspoons dried
½ teaspoon finely cracked black	2 egg yolks
pepper	1 tablespoon water
1 tablespoon finely chopped	1 tablespoon cold butter
shallots	Salt and freshly ground pepper

1. Place the one-half pound butter in a saucepan and let it melt gradually over low heat.

2. Meanwhile, combine the vinegar, pepper, and shallots and two teaspoons of the chopped fresh tarragon (or one teaspoon dried). Cook over low heat until the vinegar has evaporated. Let the saucepan cool briefly.

3. Add the egg yolks and water to the saucepan containing the shallot mixture and start beating vigorously with a wire whisk. Place over low heat and continue beating rapidly until yolks start to thicken. Take care that they do not get too hot or they will cook. Beat in the tablespoon of cold butter and remove from the heat.

4. Tilt the pan with the hot melted butter and gradually add the golden, clear liquid, spoonful by spoonful, to the egg-yolk mixture, beating rapidly with the whisk. Continue beating until all the golden liquid is added. Discard the thin milky liquid that settles on the bottom.

5. Line another saucepan with cheesecloth and scrape the sauce into it. Squeeze the sauce through the cheesecloth and into the pan. Beat in the remaining chopped tarragon and salt and pepper to taste.

Hollandaise Sauce

About 1 cup

1 cup melted, clarified butter (see below)	Pinch of cayenne pepper
	Salt to taste
2 egg yolks	1 tablespoon lemon juice, or to
2 tablespoons hot water	taste

1. It will facilitate things if you have the clarified butter in a measuring cup with a pouring spout.

2. Place the yolks and hot water in a heavy saucepan. Place over very low heat and beat the yolks vigorously with a wire whisk. Heat gently, stirring constantly, until yolks become custard-like.

3. Gradually add the butter in a steady stream. Continue until sauce is thickened and all the butter is used. Add cayenne, salt, and lemon juice.

How to clarify butter

Place butter in the top of a double boiler over hot water. Place over heat and let stand just until the butter melts. When the whey (milky sediment) has separated from the melted fat, pour off the clear fat, which is the clarified butter, and discard the whey. Half a pound of butter melted equals one cup.

Mayonnaise

About ½ cup

1 egg yolk
1 teaspoon imported prepared
   mustard, preferably Dijon or
   Düsseldorf
Salt and freshly ground pepper
   to taste

Pinch of cayenne pepper
1½ teaspoons white vinegar
1 cup peanut oil
Lemon juice

1. Place the egg yolk in a mixing bowl. Add the mustard, salt, pepper, cayenne, and vinegar. Start beating with a wire whisk, gradually adding the peanut oil.

2. Beat in lemon juice to taste. Taste for seasoning and beat in more salt, cayenne, or lemon juice, if desired.

Sauce Gribiche

*(A mayonnaise sauce with herbs
and sieved hard-cooked egg)*

About 2 cups

1 egg yolk
1 tablespoon imported prepared
   mustard, such as Dijon or
   Düsseldorf
1 tablespoon wine vinegar
1½ cups peanut, vegetable, or
   corn oil
Salt and freshly ground pepper
   to taste

1 hard-cooked egg, put through
   a sieve
1 teaspoon finely chopped onion
2 tablespoons finely chopped
   shallots
1 tablespoon finely chopped
   parsley
1 tablespoon finely chopped tarragon

Put the yolk into a mixing bowl and add the mustard and vinegar. Gradually add the oil, beating constantly and vigorously with a wire whisk. When thickened and smooth, beat and stir in the remaining ingredients.

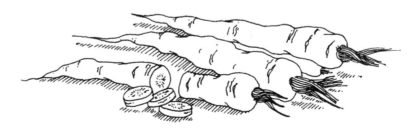

Mornay Sauce

About 5 cups

4 tablespoons butter
6 tablespoons flour
3 cups milk
⅔ cup heavy cream
Salt and freshly ground pepper

2 cups grated Gruyère or Swiss
 cheese
2 egg yolks
¼ teaspoon ground nutmeg

1. Melt the butter in a saucepan and add the flour, stirring with a wire whisk. When blended, add the milk and cream, stirring rapidly with the whisk. Season with salt and pepper to taste.

2. Add the cheese and let it melt. Bring to the boil.

3. Add the egg yolks, stirring rapidly with the whisk. Bring just to the boil and remove from the heat. Stir in the nutmeg.

Sauce Diable I

(Mustard sauce)

About ¾ cup

1 tablespoon finely chopped
 shallots
5 tablespoons dry white wine
1 cup sauce reserved from the
 braised calf's tongues
 (page 181)
1 or 2 whole hot dried red
 chilies

1 teaspoon cornstarch
Salt and freshly ground pepper
 to taste
1 tablespoon imported prepared
 mustard, such as Dijon or
 Düsseldorf
1 tablespoon cold butter

1. Combine the shallots and four tablespoons of the wine in a saucepan and bring to the boil. Reduce until very little wine is left.

2. Add the reserved sauce and chilies and bring to the boil. Blend the cornstarch and one tablespoon wine and stir it in. Cook until the sauce is reduced to about three-fourths cup.

3. Remove from the heat and stir in the mustard. Swirl in the cold butter. Do not cook further.

Sauce Diable II

About ½ cup

⅓ cup commercially prepared
 Escoffier sauce diable, available in specialty food stores
1 teaspoon imported prepared
 mustard, such as Dijon or
 Düsseldorf

2 tablespoons heavy cream
1 teaspoon Worcestershire sauce
Salt and freshly ground pepper
 to taste

Combine all the ingredients in a saucepan and bring to the boil, stirring. Serve hot.

Beurre Noisette

(Hazelnut butter)

Add any given amount of butter to a small skillet. Cook over moderate
heat, shaking the skillet so that the butter browns evenly. At first the
butter will foam. This will subside. When the butter becomes hazelnut
brown, remove it from the heat immediately and spoon over the veal.

Chive Butter

About ½ cup

4 tablespoons butter
Juice of half a lemon
Salt and freshly ground pepper
 to taste

3 tablespoons finely chopped
 chives

Heat the butter in a saucepan and add the remaining ingredients.
Bring to the simmer and serve.

Horseradish Sauce

About 1¾ cups

2 tablespoons butter
3 tablespoons flour
1 cup Veal Broth (page 197)
½ cup heavy cream
Salt and freshly ground pepper
 to taste

3 tablespoons freshly grated
 horseradish, or according to
 taste
Pinch of cayenne pepper
¼ teaspoon grated nutmeg

Melt the butter in a saucepan and add the flour, stirring with a wire whisk. When blended and smooth, add the broth, stirring rapidly with the whisk. Add the cream, salt, pepper, horseradish, cayenne, and nutmeg and stir to blend.

Tomato Sauce I

About 2 cups

2 tablespoons peanut, vegetable, or corn oil
½ cup finely chopped onion
1 teaspoon finely minced garlic
½ teaspoon dried basil
½ teaspoon dried thyme
¼ cup tomato paste
1 teaspoon flour

1 cup Veal Broth (page 197) or chicken broth
1 cup canned Italian plum tomatoes, preferably imported
Salt and freshly ground pepper to taste
1 tablespoon butter

1. Heat the oil in a saucepan and add the onion and garlic. Cook, stirring, about three minutes, or until onion is translucent. Add the basil, thyme, and tomato paste. Stir about one minute and add the flour.

2. Add the broth, stirring constantly until the mixture is thickened and smooth. Add the tomatoes, salt, and pepper and cook, partly covered, about fifteen minutes. Put the sauce through a food mill. Swirl in the tablespoon butter and serve hot.

Tomato Sauce II

About 3 cups

5 cups tomatoes
4 tablespoons butter
3 tablespoons chopped onion

1 clove garlic, finely minced
Salt and freshly ground pepper

1. Put the tomatoes through a food mill or chop them finely.

2. Melt one tablespoon butter in a saucepan and add the onion and garlic. Cook until wilted. Add the tomatoes and salt and pepper to taste and bring to the boil. Cook, stirring often, until the sauce has been reduced to about three cups.

3. Swirl in the remaining butter and serve piping hot.

Tomato Sauce III

About 3 cups

2 tablespoons olive oil
6 tablespoons butter
1½ cups chopped onions
1 tablespoon chopped garlic
¼ pound mushrooms, finely
  chopped
¾ cup finely chopped carrots
2 tablespoons finely chopped
  fresh parsley
1 tablespoon finely chopped
  fresh basil or 1 teaspoon
  dried

6 sprigs fresh thyme or 1 teaspoon dried
1 teaspoon sugar
1 whole clove
½ cup dry white wine
4 cups chopped fresh or canned
  tomatoes
Salt and freshly ground pepper
  to taste

1. Heat the oil and two tablespoons of butter in a heavy casserole and add the onions, garlic, mushrooms, carrots, parsley, basil, thyme, sugar, and clove. Cook, stirring, until the mixture is almost dry but still moist, about ten minutes.

2. Add the wine and cook, stirring, over high heat until wine evaporates. Add the tomatoes, salt, and pepper and bring to the boil. Partly cover and simmer one hour.

3. Put the mixture through a food mill, pushing through as much of the vegetable solids as possible. Stir in the remaining butter and bring to the boil.

Primavera Sauce

(A light, fresh tomato-and-basil sauce)

3 cups

3 pounds red, ripe tomatoes
3 tablespoons olive oil
3 tablespoons finely chopped
  garlic
Salt and freshly ground pepper
  to taste

2 tablespoons finely chopped
  parsley
2 tablespoons finely chopped
  basil

1. Peel, core, and chop the tomatoes.

2. Heat the oil and add the garlic. Cook briefly, without browning, and add the tomatoes, salt, and pepper. Add the parsley and basil and bring to the boil. Simmer about five minutes, stirring to make certain the sauce does not stick.

Sauce Belle Aurore

(A tomato-with-cream sauce)

About 3 cups

4 tablespoons butter
2 tablespoons finely chopped
  onion
1 tablespoon finely chopped
  shallots
½ teaspoon chopped garlic
¼ cup flour
2 cups Veal Broth (page 197) or
  chicken broth

¾ cup drained, chopped tomatoes
1 small dried hot red pepper
  (optional)
Salt and freshly ground pepper
  to taste
¾ cup heavy cream
⅛ teaspoon grated nutmeg
1 tablespoon Cognac

1. Melt half the butter in a saucepan and add the onion, shallots, and garlic. Cook, stirring, until onions are wilted.

2. Sprinkle with flour, stirring with a wire whisk. When blended, add the veal broth, tomatoes, hot pepper, salt, and pepper. Cook fifteen minutes.

3. Add the cream. Simmer fifteen minutes, stirring often. Add the nutmeg.

4. Cook ten minutes longer. Put the mixture through a fine sieve, preferably the one known in French as a chinois. Push to extract as much liquid from the solids as possible.

5. Swirl in the remaining butter and add the Cognac.

Sour Cream, Dill, and Tomato Sauce

About 1½ cups

1 tablespoon butter
2 tablespoons finely chopped
  onion
1 cup diced fresh tomatoes or
  drained canned tomatoes

Salt and freshly ground pepper
  to taste
Pan juices from veal loaf (page 131)
1 cup sour cream
1 tablespoon chopped fresh dill

1. Melt the butter in a saucepan or small skillet and add the onion. Cook until wilted. Add the tomatoes, salt, and pepper and cook about five minutes.

2. Skim off the fat from the veal-loaf pan juices and add them to the sauce. Add the sour cream and dill and bring just to the boil, stirring. Serve hot.

Creole Sauce

About 3½ cups

1 tablespoon butter
1½ cups finely chopped onion
1 clove garlic, finely minced
½ cup finely chopped celery
¾ cup finely chopped sweet
  green and/or red peppers
2 cups (about ¼ pound) thinly
  sliced mushrooms
1 dried hot pepper, or dried red
  pepper flakes to taste (optional)

2 cups chopped canned im-
  ported tomatoes
½ cup Veal Broth (page 197) or
  chicken broth
Salt and freshly ground pepper
1 tablespoon cornstarch
2 tablespoons water
3 tablespoons finely chopped
  parsley

1. Heat the butter in a casserole and add the onion, garlic, celery, sweet peppers, and mushrooms. Cook, stirring often, about five minutes.

2. Add the hot pepper, tomatoes, veal broth, salt, and pepper. Bring to the boil and simmer about ten minutes. Blend the cornstarch and water and add it. Let simmer about five minutes longer. Stir in the parsley and serve.

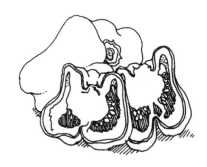

•Accompaniments•

Chefs and epicures have known for centuries that there are thousands of flavors and textures that "marry" well with various other foods. Thus it is that in this book there are certain dishes that for empirical reasons complement dishes made with veal. Many of them are noodle-based, such as buttered fine noodles, macaroni au gratin, and spaetzle; rice with certain veal dishes is as natural as puréed potatoes and polenta. And braised celery, fennel, or endives are highly recommended side dishes for many of the recipes found in this book.

Buttered Fine Noodles

8 servings

8 ounces fine noodles
3 tablespoons butter at room
  temperature
Salt and freshly ground pepper
  to taste

¼ teaspoon grated nutmeg or
  more to taste

1. Drop the noodles into boiling water and, when the water returns to the boil, cook six or eight minutes. Drain in a colander, then empty into a hot dish.

2. Add the butter and toss until evenly distributed. Add salt, pepper, and nutmeg. Toss quickly and serve hot.

Macaroni au Gratin

8 or more servings

1 pound "ready-cut" macaroni,
  elbow macaroni, or ziti
7 tablespoons butter
Salt and freshly ground pepper
  to taste

¾ pound grated Swiss or
  Gruyère cheese, about three
  cups
1 cup piping hot cream
1 cup piping hot milk

1. Preheat the oven to 400 degrees.

2. Cook the macaroni according to package directions. Do not overcook, for it will cook further on baking.

3. Drain the macaroni well and return it to a kettle. Add four tablespoons of butter, salt, pepper, and half the cheese. Toss to blend.

4. Grease a baking dish (one measuring 14 x 8 x 1½ inches is suitable) with one tablespoon of butter. Add the macaroni in an even layer. Pour the hot cream and milk over all and sprinkle with the remaining cheese. Dot with two tablespoons of butter and bake twenty minutes.

5. Run under the broiler to glaze.

Spaetzle

(Egg dumplings)

4 to 6 servings

2 cups sifted flour	Salt to taste
2 eggs	2 tablespoons butter
⅔ cup milk	

1. Place the flour in a mixing bowl. Beat the eggs and add them to the flour, stirring with a wire whisk or an electric beater. Gradually add the milk, beating or stirring constantly. Add salt.

2. Bring a large quantity of water to the boil in a kettle and add salt to taste. Pour the spaetzle mixture into a colander and hold the colander over the boiling water. Press the noodle mixture through the holes of the colander with a rubber spatula or large spoon. Cook until the noodles rise to the surface. Drain and spoon them onto paper towels to dry.

3. Heat the butter in a skillet and cook the spaetzle, tossing and stirring, three to five minutes. Serve hot.

Spaghetti with Marinara Sauce

8 servings

4 cups imported Italian tomatoes	1 tablespoon chopped fresh
Salt and freshly ground pepper	basil or 1 teaspoon dried
¼ teaspoon sugar (optional)	1 pound spaghetti
2 tablespoons olive oil	Freshly grated Parmesan cheese
1 clove garlic, finely chopped	

1. Empty the tomatoes with their liquid into a heavy saucepan. Bring to the boil and simmer until the tomatoes are reduced to three cups. If you want a thicker sauce, which is preferable, let the tomatoes cook until they are reduced to two cups. Stir frequently from the bottom so that the tomatoes do not stick to the pan.

2. Add salt and pepper to taste and, if desired, sugar.

3. Heat the olive oil in a saucepan. Add the garlic and cook for a few seconds. Add the tomato sauce and stir with a wire whisk until the oil is thoroughly blended with the sauce. Add the basil.

4. Serve with cooked spaghetti and grated Parmesan cheese.

Baked Rice

8 to 12 servings

5 tablespoons butter
¼ cup minced onion
½ teaspoon minced garlic
2 cups uncooked rice
3 cups Veal Broth (page 197) or
    chicken broth

3 sprigs parsley
2 sprigs fresh thyme or ½ tea-
    spoon dried
1 bay leaf
¼ teaspoon cayenne pepper or
    Tabasco to taste

1. Preheat the oven to 400 degrees.

2. Melt two tablespoons of the butter in a heavy saucepan and cook the onion and garlic, stirring with a wooden spoon, until the onion is translucent. Add the rice and stir briefly over low heat until the grains are coated with butter.

3. Stir in the broth, making sure there are no lumps in the rice. Add the parsley, thyme, bay leaf, and cayenne. Cover with a close-fitting lid and place in the oven.

4. Bake the rice exactly seventeen minutes. Remove the cover and discard the parsley and thyme sprigs. Using a two-pronged fork, stir in the remaining butter. Like most dishes, this rice is best if served as soon as it is baked. But it may be made as much as half an hour in advance as long as it is kept tightly covered and warm.

Baked Rice with Herbs and Spices

Saffron rice: To the basic recipe for baked rice, add one teaspoon stem saffron, loosely packed, along with the bay leaf.

Curried rice: In the basic recipe for baked rice, sprinkle the cooked onion and garlic with one or two teaspoons of curry powder before adding the rice.

Parsleyed rice: When the basic recipe for baked rice is cooked, stir in a tablespoon of chopped parsley when adding the remaining butter.

Kashmiri Rice

(Saffron rice with currants)

8 servings

3 tablespoons butter
2 tablespoons finely chopped
   onion
1½ cups long-grain rice
2¼ cups Veal Broth (page 197)
   or chicken broth

¼ cup currants
1 strip of lemon peel
1 bay leaf
½ teaspoon stem saffron
Salt to taste

1. Preheat the oven to 400 degrees.

2. Use a heavy saucepan with a tight-fitting lid. Melt one tablespoon butter in the saucepan and add the onion. Cook, stirring, until onion is wilted. Add the rice and cook, stirring, about thirty seconds. Add the remaining ingredients except butter and bring to a boil.

3. Cover and place the saucepan in the oven. Cook exactly seventeen minutes. Uncover and stir. Keep covered until ready to serve. Discard the bay leaf. Fluff the rice with a fork and stir in the remaining butter.

Risotto

8 servings

6 tablespoons butter
3 tablespoons finely chopped
   onion
1 clove garlic, finely minced
2 cups raw rice
Salt and freshly ground pepper
   to taste

1 teaspoon chopped stem saffron
5 cups Veal Broth (page 197) or
   chicken broth
½ cup dry white wine
¾ cup freshly grated Parmesan
   cheese

1. Heat two tablespoons of butter in a fairly large casserole. Add the onion and garlic and cook until onion is wilted. Add the rice, salt, pepper, and saffron and stir to coat the grains.

2. Meanwhile, heat the broth and keep it at the simmer.

3. Add the wine to the rice and cook, stirring occasionally, until all the wine has evaporated.

4. Add one cup of the hot broth to the rice mixture and cook, stirring occasionally and gently, until all that liquid has been absorbed. Add one-half cup more of the broth and cook, stirring occasionally, until it is absorbed. Continue cooking the rice in this fashion, adding half a cup of broth each three or four minutes, just until each ladle is absorbed. Remember that the rice must cook gently.

5. When all the broth has been added and absorbed, fold in the remaining butter and the cheese. When the rice is done, the grains should be tender except at the very core, which should retain a very small bite. The total cooking time should be from twenty-five to twenty-eight minutes.

Cold Rice Salad

6 servings

1 cup uncooked rice
2 tomatoes, peeled
1½ cups cooked, unbuttered
   peas
1 green pepper, cored, seeded,
   and chopped fine
¼ cup finely chopped green
   onion, including green part

½ cup Mayonnaise (page 200)
1 tablespoon chopped fresh
   basil
1 teaspoon chopped fresh mint
Salt and freshly ground pepper
   to taste.

1. Cook the rice according to package directions and chill. The grains should be tender yet firm and dry.

2. Gently squeeze the liquid and seeds from the tomatoes into a sieve over a mixing bowl. Reserve this liquid, discarding the seeds. Chop the tomatoes.

3. Combine the rice, tomatoes, peas, green pepper, and green onion.

4. Stir the mayonnaise into the reserved tomato juice and mix well. Add the mayonnaise mixture to the rice, toss together with the herbs, and add salt and pepper to taste.

Puréed Potatoes

About 6 servings

2 pounds potatoes
Salt to taste
1 cup milk

4 tablespoons butter, at room
   temperature
¼ teaspoon nutmeg, or to taste

1. Peel the potatoes and quarter them, or cut them into two-inch cubes.

2. Place the potatoes in a saucepan and add cold water to cover and salt to taste. Bring to the boil and simmer twenty minutes, or until potatoes are tender.

3. Drain the potatoes and put them through a food mill or potato ricer. Return them to the saucepan.

4. Meanwhile, bring the milk to the boil.

5. While the milk is being heated, use a wooden spoon and add the butter to the potatoes while beating. Add salt and nutmeg to taste and beat in the hot milk.

Skillet Potatoes

6 servings

1½ to 2 pounds potatoes
¼ cup peanut, vegetable, or corn oil
6 tablespoons butter
Salt and freshly ground pepper to taste

1. Preheat the oven to 400 degrees.

2. Peel and slice the potatoes thin and drop the slices into cold water. Drain. Drop them into cold water to cover and bring to the boil. Simmer four minutes and drain well.

3. Add the oil and four tablespoons of butter to a ten-inch skillet and, when the butter is melted and the oil very hot, add the potatoes in neat layers. Sprinkle with salt and pepper.

4. Bake the potatoes about fifteen minutes, or until golden brown on the bottom. Carefully turn them in the skillet, preferably keeping the crust intact. Bake twenty minutes longer, or until golden brown on the other side. Brush with remaining two tablespoons of butter, melted, and serve.

Potatoes in Cream Sauce

6 to 8 servings

6 potatoes, about 2½ pounds, unpeeled
Salt to taste
4 tablespoons butter
Freshly ground pepper to taste
¼ teaspoon grated nutmeg
2 cups milk
1 cup heavy cream

1. Rinse the potatoes in their skins and put them in a large saucepan. Add cold water to cover and salt to taste. Bring to the boil and simmer thirty minutes, or until tender but not mushy. Let cool in the water.

2. Peel the potatoes. Split them in half lengthwise, then cut each half into slices slightly more than a quarter inch thick.

3. Butter a heavy skillet with the four tablespoons of butter and arrange the potatoes in layers in the skillet. Sprinkle with salt, pepper, and nutmeg. Add the milk and cream. The dish may be left at this point until half an hour before serving time.

4. Thirty minutes before serving, put the potatoes on the stove and cook over low heat twenty-five to thirty minutes. As the potatoes cook, shake the skillet gently, but do not stir or the slices will break.

Purée of Celery Root

6 to 8 servings

1½ pounds potatoes
¾ pound firm knob celery
Salt to taste
1 cup milk

4 tablespoons butter
¼ teaspoon grated nutmeg, or
  to taste

1. Peel and quarter the potatoes and drop into a kettle or deep saucepan.

2. Peel the knob celery, removing and discarding all the brown exterior. Rinse well and cut into large slices or cubes. Add to the potatoes. Add water to cover and salt to taste and bring to the boil. Simmer twenty to thirty minutes, or until vegetables are tender.

3. Meanwhile, bring the milk to the boil.

4. Put the potatoes and celery through a fine food mill or a potato ricer. Add the butter and beat it in with a wooden spoon. Add the nutmeg and gradually add the hot milk, beating with the spoon. Serve immediately or place the dish in a basin of simmering water and keep warm.

Polenta

(Corn-meal mush)

8 to 12 servings

9½ cups water
2 tablespoons butter
Salt to taste

2 cups yellow corn meal, preferably imported, available in
  Italian grocery stores

1. Put the water in a large kettle and add the butter and salt. Bring to the boil.

2. Add the corn meal gradually, a handful at a time, stirring constantly. The best utensil to stir this with is a thin wooden rolling pin.

3. Stir the mixture almost constantly for forty to fifty minutes. Serve hot.

Braised Fennel

4 to 8 servings

4 medium unblemished fennel
  bulbs
7 tablespoons butter
1½ cups Veal Broth (page 197)
  or chicken broth

Salt and freshly ground pepper
  to taste
1½ cups grated Gruyère or
  Swiss cheese

1. Preheat the oven to 400 degrees.

2. Cut each fennel bulb into halves. If the outer leaves seem tough, pull them off and discard.

3. Layer the pieces, cut side down, in a casserole. Dot with three table-spoons of butter and add the veal broth. Add salt and pepper to taste and bring to the boil on top of the stove. Cover closely and place the casserole in the oven. Bake twenty-five to thirty minutes, or until tender yet firm. They must not become mushy. Drain.

4. Cut each piece in half and arrange the quarters in one layer, cut side up, in a baking dish. Sprinkle with cheese and pour the remaining four tablespoons of butter, melted, over all. Bake ten minutes, then run the dish under the broiler until cheese becomes golden brown.

Braised Endives

4 servings

12 small endives
5 tablespoons butter
Juice of ½ lemon

1 teaspoon salt
⅓ cup water
1 teaspoon sugar

1. Trim off and discard any discolored leaves from the outside of the endives. Place the heads in a kettle and add two tablespoons of the but-ter and the lemon juice, salt, water, and sugar. Cover and bring to the boil. Cook over moderate heat for thirty to forty minutes, until endives are tender.

2. Drain the endives and press gently to remove any excess moisture.

3. Heat the remaining butter in a large skillet and brown the endives on all sides. They should be a light caramel color when cooked.

Braised Celery

4 to 6 servings

6 celery hearts
2 tablespoons olive oil
2 tablespoons butter
Salt and freshly ground pepper
    to taste

½ cup dry white wine
¼ cup Veal Broth (page 197) or
    chicken broth

1. Cut off most of the leaves and remove the rough outer ribs of the celery. Cut each heart lengthwise into halves. Wash thoroughly and drain on paper towels.

2. Heat the oil and butter in a skillet large enough to hold all the celery pieces in one layer. Arrange the pieces, flat side down, in the skillet and cook over low heat until lightly browned. Turn the pieces and sprinkle with salt and pepper. Brown the rounded side, turn, and sprinkle with salt and pepper. Add more oil and butter to the skillet if it becomes too dry.

3. Pour the wine and broth into the pan, cover, and simmer gently until the celery is tender. Remove the celery to a heated serving plate. Reduce the cooking liquid a little and spoon some of it over the celery.

Grilled Tomatoes with Oregano

8 to 10 servings

5 large, red, ripe tomatoes
1 tablespoon plus 10 teaspoons
    peanut, vegetable, or corn oil
5 teaspoons chopped fresh or
    dried oregano

Salt and freshly ground pepper
    to taste

1. Preheat the broiler.

2. Core the tomatoes and slice them in half.

3. Grease a baking dish large enough to hold the tomato halves with one tablespoon of oil. Arrange the halves over it, cut side up.

4. Sprinkle each half with about half a teaspoon of chopped oregano, salt, and pepper. Sprinkle about one teaspoon oil over each half and place them under the broiler. Broil about five minutes.

Carrots Vichy

6 servings

1½ pounds carrots, trimmed
   and scraped
Salt and freshly ground pepper
   to taste

1 teaspoon sugar
¼ cup water
4 tablespoons butter
Chopped parsley

1. Cut the carrots into very thin rounds. There should be about four cups. Put them in a skillet and add salt, pepper, sugar, water (Vichy water if you want to be authentic), and butter.

2. Cover with a round of buttered wax paper and cook over moderately high heat, shaking the skillet occasionally. Cook about ten minutes, until carrots are tender, the liquid has disappeared, and they are lightly glazed. Take care they do not burn. Serve sprinkled with chopped parsley.

Creamed Spinach

4 to 6 servings

2½ pounds fresh spinach in
   bulk or 2 10-ounce packages
2 cups water
5 tablespoons butter
2 tablespoons flour
1 cup milk

Salt and freshly ground pepper
   to taste
⅛ teaspoon grated nutmeg or
   more to taste
¼ cup heavy cream

1. Trim off the stems of the spinach. Wash the spinach in several changes of cold water to remove any traces of sand. Drain.

2. Bring two cups of water to the boil and add the spinach. Cook, turning the spinach over with a two-pronged fork until it is wilted. Cook about three minutes and drain. Rinse the spinach under cold running water and drain again. Squeeze to extract most of the moisture. There should be about one cup of firmly packed spinach.

3. Chop the spinach as finely as possible or put into the container of an electric blender and blend, stirring down as necessary. Do not add liquid.

4. Melt two tablespoons of butter and add the flour, stirring with a wire whisk. Add the milk, stirring rapidly with the whisk. Add salt and pepper to taste and the nutmeg.

5. Heat one tablespoon of butter in a saucepan and add the spinach and the sauce, stirring to blend. Add the cream and salt and pepper to taste. Add the remaining butter, stir it in, and serve piping hot.

Endives au Gratin

8 servings

16 large endives
3 tablespoons butter
Juice of ½ lemon
Salt and freshly ground pepper
  to taste

½ cup freshly grated Parmesan
  cheese
¼ cup melted butter

1. Trim a thin slice off the bottom of each endive. Place the endives in a heavy casserole and add the butter and lemon. If the casserole is heavy enough, it is not necessary to add water. Otherwise, add one-third cup water. Add salt and pepper and cover closely. Simmer thirty to forty minutes, or until vegetable is tender. Drain, then squeeze each endive lightly to extract excess moisture.

2. Preheat the oven to 400 degrees.

3. Arrange the endives on a buttered baking dish just large enough to hold them in one layer. Sprinkle with cheese and pour the butter over all. Bake thirty minutes. Serve hot.

Asparagus Milanaise

6 servings

3 pounds fresh asparagus (36 to
  42 stalks, depending on size)
Salt and freshly ground pepper
  to taste

½ cup grated Parmesan cheese
2 tablespoons butter

1. Use a potato peeler and scrape the asparagus spears to within two inches of the top. Cut off and discard the tough bottoms of the spears to make them of uniform length. Place stalks in a skillet and add cold water to cover and salt. Bring to the boil and simmer until tender yet firm.

2. Preheat the broiler.

3. Drain the asparagus and arrange them on a heatproof, buttered baking dish. Sprinkle with salt and pepper, then with the cheese. Dot with butter.

4. Run under the broiler for one to three minutes until cheese is golden brown.

TABLE OF EQUIVALENTS
(Volume and Weight)

Volume (common units)

1 ounce	28.35 grams
1 pound	453.59 grams
1 gram	0.035 ounces
1 kilogram	2.21 pounds

Weight (common units)

1 cup	16 tablespoons
	8 fluid ounces
	236.6 milliliters
1 tablespoon	3 teaspoons
	0.5 fluid ounce
	14.8 milliliters
1 teaspoon	4.9 milliliters
1 liter	1,000 milliliters
	1.06 quarts
1 bushel	4 pecks
1 peck	8 quarts
1 gallon	4 quarts
1 quart	2 pints
1 pint	2 cups
	473.2 milliliters

INDEX